Governors State University
Library Hours:
Monday thru Thursday 8:00 to 10:30
Friday 8:00 to 5:00
Saturday 8:30 to 5:00
Sunday 1:00 to 5:00 (Fall
and Winter Trimester Only)

the series on school reform

Patricia A. Wasley
University
of Washington

Ann Lieberman
Carnegie Foundation for the
Advancement of Teaching

Joseph P. McDonald
New York
University

SERIES EDITORS

(Continued)

the series on school reform, *continued*

Teaching the Way Children Learn

BEVERLY FALK

Teachers College
Columbia University
New York and London

Great Public Schools for Every Child

NEA Professional Library
National Education Association
Washington, D.C.

This work was supported by generous grants from the American Educational Research Association and the Professional Staff Congress of The City University of New York, 2002–2004

Sections of Chapter 3 are adapted from Falk, B. (January 12, 2006). Morning meeting. *ASCD Express, 1*(7). Copyright © 2006 by ASCD. Used with permission. Learn more about ASCD at www.ascd.org.

Sections of Chapter 11 are adapted from Lieberman, A., & Falk, B. (2006). Leadership in learner-centered schools. In Danzig, A. B., Borman, K. M., Jones, B. A., & Wright, W.F. (Eds.), *Learner-Centered Leadership: Research, Policy, and Practice*. Mahwah, NJ: Lawrence Erlbaum. Copyright © 2006 by Taylor and Francis Group LLC. Used by permission of Taylor and Francis Group LLC.

In Chapter 8, the poem "Children Learn What They Live" has been excerpted from the book *Children Learn What They Live* by Dorothy Law Nolte and Rachel Harris. The poem "Children Learn What They Live" is copyright © 1972 by Dorothy Law Nolte and is used by permission of Workman Publishing Co., Inc., New York. All rights reserved.

Published simultaneously by Teachers College Press, 1234 Amsterdam Avenue, New York, NY 10027 and the NEA Professional Library, 1201 16th Street N.W., Washington, D.C. 20036.

Note: The opinions expressed in this publication should not be construed as representing the policy or position of the National Education Association. Materials published by the NEA Professional Library are intended to be discussion documents for educators who are concerned with specialized interests of the profession.

Library of Congress Cataloging-in-Publication Data

Falk, Beverly.
  Teaching the way children learn / Beverly Falk.
    p. cm.
  Includes bibliographical references and index.
  ISBN 978-0-8077-4928-9 (pbk. : alk. paper)
  ISBN 978-0-8077-4929-6 (hardcover : alk. paper)
    1. Active learning—United States. 2. Constructivism (Education)—United States. 3. Critical thinking—United States. 4. Teaching—United States. I. Title.
  LB1027.23.F35 2009
  372.1102–dc22   2008038991

Teachers College ISBN 978-0-8077-4928-9 (paper)
Teachers College ISBN 978-0-8077-4929-6 (hardcover)

National Education Association ISBN: 978-0-8106-1877-0 (paper)

Printed on acid-free paper

Manufactured in the United States of America

16   15   14   13   12   11   10   09   8   7   6   5   4   3   2   1

Contents

PART II
IMAGES OF POSSIBILITY: TEACHING

PART III
IMAGES OF POSSIBILITY:
SCHOOLWIDE STRUCTURES AND PRACTICES

Acknowledgments

Over the past 35 years I have had the privilege of working with educators and schools all over the United States that have struggled with the challenges of teaching children from diverse backgrounds in the ways that they learn. However, the experience of creating and working with the Bronx New School (P.S. 51 in New York City's Community School District 10) has been one of the most enriching of these and holds a very special place in my heart. I am grateful to all the children, families, teachers, staff, and administrators—both past and present—who have been a part of the school's history. They have demonstrated what it means to be active, concerned citizens of our democracy who, by joining in community with others, can make a difference in theirs and others' lives. I am particularly indebted to those whose work is featured in the different chapters of this book: Martha Andrews, Susan Gordon, Sue MacMurdy, Ronnie Ranere, and Paul Smith. Thanks also to Althea Jervis, Karen Khan, Kendra Sibley, Sasha Wilson, and other Bronx New School faculty and staff whose practices are referred to in the text.

The influence of many colleagues is evident in the ideas I have expressed throughout. They have stretched my thinking, deepened my understanding, and inspired me over the years. These include those with whom I have worked closely and those whose writings and work have touched me from afar—Patricia Carini, Linda Darling-Hammond, Eleanor Duckworth, Paolo Freire, Gloria Ladson-Billings, Ann Lieberman, Deborah Meier, Sonia Nieto, Raymond Pecheone, and Lillian Weber. In addition, I am most appreciative of my colleagues at the Carnegie Foundation for the Advancement of Teaching—Sharon Feiman-Nemser, Tom Hatch, Ann Lieberman, Désirée Pointer-Mace, Anna Richert, and Lee Shulman—whose stimulating conversations and provocative questions during the time I was a fellow of the foundation's Quest Project helped me to process some of the evidence I collected for this book and to frame how I wanted to present it.

My editors at Teachers College Press—Marie Ellen Larcada, Wendy Schwartz, and Shannon Waite—offered me thoughtful critique

and helpful suggestions that have enhanced the coherence and read-
ability of this text. I thank them for their faith in my abilities and
their friendship and support throughout our collaboration.

Most of all, I want to express my love and gratitude to my family—
Alan, Luba, Meryl, Anaiya, Thabiti, and Frank—for their steady love
and support as well as for the many ways they are contributing to making the world a more just place. It is to possibilities for them and all
children in the future that I dedicate this book.

Introduction

On her first day of kindergarten, my older daughter and I said good-bye at the gate to her school's outdoor yard. There she was instructed to join with her 5-year-old classmates and line up in silent size-place rows, one for the girls and one for the boys. Parents were not permitted to enter the yard to help ease the children's transition. Because of this we couldn't help them understand why the adult in charge was shouting at them through a bullhorn in a space not much larger than a living room.

This was the beginning of many things about school that I wasn't able to explain to my daughter. Despite the fact that she was going to what was considered a "good school"—a well-kept building with a big playground, situated in a lovely, albeit modest, green neighborhood; spotless floors, freshly painted walls, neatly arranged bulletin boards, and decent test scores; and a safe environment, in contrast with the abysmal conditions of other schools in the same district (which had been written about during this time by Jonathan Kozol [1991] in his searing book, *Savage Inequalities*)—the school made my stomach ache.

Some of what I learned, as the days went by, helped me to understand why I felt that way. I found out that classes were "tracked" by ability levels. The top class, which my daughter was in, turned out to be populated by mostly White, middle-class children, and the "lower-track" classes were filled predominantly by children of color from low-income neighborhoods. This, of course, determined whom she knew, the friends she made, whom she sat with in the lunchroom and played with at recess. Despite the fact that her dad and I had sent her to this school to be in an integrated public setting, the reality of her experience was actually quite segregated.

Over time, there were other upsetting facts that I learned about my daughter's school. When I visited during lunch or recess, I found the atmosphere chaotic and the noise overwhelming. Little was provided for the children to do, and when they got restless, which they inevitably did, the adults would shout at them to be quiet or sit still.

The latter's disdain was revealed through the tone of their voices or comments, such as one I overheard: "These children act like animals." Classroom life, while quieter and more orderly, had an uncannily similar feel. For much of the day, children were required to sit at their desks. Whole-group instruction and worksheets were the norm; doing the same thing at the same time, the general rule.

Memories stand out: When Luba (my daughter) was in the first grade, she came home with her first homework assignment—to complete several workbook pages of letter and sound identification tasks. The skills in the book were required to be "mastered" before the children could be taught to "read." The fact that Luba was already a fluent reader didn't exempt her from the assignment. "I'm learning how to read all over again, Mommy," she cheerily explained as she climbed onto a chair at the dining room table and busily proceeded to complete the entire book in one night.

Some of Luba's peers, however, did not accept their lot so good-naturedly. Turned off by the "one size fits all" teaching that prevailed, finding little validation for strengths they possessed that didn't pertain directly to reading or math, many of them were unable to find a way to be successful. As a result, some were moved to "bottom track" classes; others simply resigned themselves to this state of affairs, gradually slipping into a state of ennui or becoming restless or defiant.

Although silence and obedience were valued so highly in this school, there were a lot of discipline problems. Children who were "bad" were punished by having to stand in a corner at the back of the classroom. When the class got too noisy or didn't follow the rules, all the children had to sit at their desks with their hands on their heads. Good behavior was rewarded with points, which children traded in for candy or toys at the end of each week. This contributed to resentment that brewed and sometimes surfaced in fights among the children. Everyone knew who was "good" and who was "bad," who was "smart" and who was not. What a contrast these experiences in "the school for big children" were with those of my daughter's happier days in early childhood classrooms, where kids mixed together in a carefree way, each known for his or her own strengths and unique qualities.

As a parent, I was dissatisfied. And as an educator—I had been the director of our neighborhood child-care center for many years—I was worried not only about my own child(!), but also, along with other neighborhood parents, about all the children who attended the school, many of whom I had earlier helped to nurture. I couldn't imagine how this rigid environment was going to support them to become engaged learners and active thinkers. Or how the behavioral constraints of this punitive atmosphere could help them become caring, compassionate, responsible adults. How could their little spirits survive?

In 1900 John Dewey wrote:

> What the best and wisest parent wants for his own child, that must the community want for all of its children. Any other ideal for our schools is narrow and unlovely; acted upon, it destroys our democracy. (1900/1956, p. 3)

In the spirit of what John Dewey wrote, I wanted all children to have an education that enhanced, rather than squelched, the human striving to learn, that was supportive of their unique ways of learning—different from adults and also individually different from those of each other, and that challenged them to achieve the highest standards in an atmosphere of diversity and equity. I wanted a school that offered the kind of active, purposeful in-depth learning found in everyday real-life experiences, a richness from which children learn so much (to walk, to speak their native language, to master the complex nuances of their cultures) all before they ever enter the schoolhouse door.

As an educator I knew that children's active involvement with materials, experiences, and social relationships nurtures their natural desire to learn. I also knew that caring adults, who consciously try to foster independence, intrinsic motivation, and kindness toward others through the words and actions they carefully choose, create a community of safety and trust in which children's self-esteem and sense of self flourishes. I had witnessed how powerfully children are affected by the moment-to-moment quality of life in a school; how the emotional tenor of adult-child interactions influences each child's sense of self-worth; how adults who know each child well and support children's interests can bring out their various and diverse strengths—intellectual, artistic, physical, social—so that they experience success. I knew that my daughter's school environment contradicted much of what I had learned and experienced.

At first I attributed some of this phenomenon to the fact that support of children's learning through the observing, recording, and analyzing of their work—the foundation of early childhood education—seemed to be largely absent in the environment of the elementary school. But I also soon realized that the problems were more complex and profound. The actions of this school, as of all others, were reflective of its values, purposes, and contexts. Typical of many elementary schools—then and now—the standardized teaching and testing atmosphere of my daughter's school had room for only a small handful of academically inclined students to be successful. It provided few avenues for the much larger group of students found in every classroom, whose strengths are manifested in different ways, to express themselves and to excel. With images of those children guiding my actions, I committed myself to the work of making schooling more responsive to diverse learners—so that children would not merely survive, but flourish, and so that all children could realize their own special potential.

This book tells the story of that work. Drawn from past and current studies of the Bronx New School—the school that I helped to found and once led—it tells a story about one community's efforts to address the challenges of preparing children to acquire strong knowledge and skills, to think critically and creatively, to apply their understandings to real-world problems, and to cultivate a sense of responsibility toward others. While partially autobiographical, what is written here is the result of systematic research about these efforts: I have observed and documented classrooms, reviewed students' work, engaged in reflective processes with educators, and talked with students and their families. My research includes a documentation of the Bronx New School's beginnings, 1987–1991; a 2002–2004 study (funded by grants from the American Educational Research Association and the Professional Staff Congress of the City University of New York), for which I returned to the Bronx New School to examine how it was negotiating its practices and structures within the constraints of current local and national policies; and a Web-based video documentation of the Bronx New School's teaching that I worked on with other colleagues in 2005–2007 while a fellow of the Quest Project of the Carnegie Foundation for the Advancement of Teaching. While the generous support of others provided the resources and opportunities that made these studies possible, the interpretations I share here are mine alone. I take full responsibility for them, including any mistakes I may have made.

All the work that will be described here takes place in the context of questions that are central to schooling in a democracy: How can we ensure that schools are equitable—that they support and are responsive to children from diverse backgrounds who possess different strengths and learning styles? How can we design learning environments that teach so that children truly make meaning of—understand and own—the knowledge and skills to which they have been exposed? How can we nurture within children a love for learning and support their imaginations, their sense of capacity as learners, their abilities to think critically and autonomously? How can we encourage them to develop empathy and social responsibility so that they can use what they know to contribute to the betterment of our human community? And how can we create assessments and systems of accountability that accurately reflect and support these valued goals?

This last question is of particular relevance because high-stakes testing and accountability policies are proliferating in the United States and other countries, increasingly threatening educators' abilities to teach in rich and fulsome ways. Ever since the 1983 report *A Nation At Risk* (National Commission on Excellence in Education) warned that American schools were failing miserably, a wave of local, state, and federal reforms have doled out punishments and rewards for students' outcomes on tests, pressing educators more and more to use standardized practices and to focus narrowly on academics, even for the very youngest students. "One size fits all" teaching methods that "teach to the test" have dominated classrooms, especially in poor, urban, and minority communities where greater percentages of students generally do not experience academic success (Au, 2007).

This approach has left many children behind, especially those, like my daughter's classmates, who, because they diverge in some way from the mainstream—by learning style, class, language, or culture—are in need of meaningful learning experiences differentiated to their varied learning styles and paces (Bransford, Brown, & Cocking, 2000). And because of the limitations of most standardized tests (multiple choice or fill-in-the-blank answer formats that allow for only one "right answer" to be expressed in only one way; questions decontextualized from the application of knowledge; timed test administrations that privilege speed over thoughtful deliberation) the information provided by them does not let children demonstrate the full range of what they know and can do and therefore is often of little use to teaching. As a result, many children do not score well on the tests and then suffer the consequences of the high stakes attached—they are kept from graduating or moving on to the next grade—escalating their risk of dropping out and narrowing their options for the future (Darling-Hammond, 1991; McNeil, 2000).

All this is happening despite opposition to the problems of standardized testing, the high stakes attached to them, and the lack of sustainable results from their use (National Association for the Education of Young Children, 1987; National Association for the Education of Young Children & National Association for Early Childhood Specialists in State Departments of Education, 2003; National Association of School Psychologists, 2005; Rothstein, 2004). This opposition is based on mounting evidence about how high-stakes testing and the test prep curricula often used to prepare for them hamper educators' abilities to provide the rich, active learning experiences that foster children's deep understanding of subject matter and to develop the very higher-order processes called for by many current standards (Datnow & Castellano, 1999; Meier & Wood, 2003; Moon, Callahan, & Tomlinson, 2003; Pogrow, 2000; Popham, 2001). In fact, since the enactment of the No Child Left Behind Act of 2001, legislation requiring yearly testing in Grades 3-8 and imposing unprecedented mandates and sanctions on children and schools, test score growth that took place in earlier decades has faded and progress toward narrowing achievement gaps has largely disappeared (Fuller, Wright, Gesicki, & Kang, 2007; Institute of Education Sciences, 2008; Krashen, 2007a, 2007b; Lee, 2006).

At the same time that these problems have arisen, there have been successful efforts to develop different, more useful approaches to accountability. These new approaches advocate support rather than punishment for those most in need and use multiple forms of more performance-oriented assessments (such as portfolios, performance tasks, observations, and performances) to examine how children apply their knowledge and skills in real-life problem-solving situations. Such assessments, when part of a standards-based system that reflects reasonable expectations for what children of different ages should accomplish, have the capacity to provide reliable information to the public as well as information that informs teaching and supports student learning (Gallagher, 2007). Such a system is what I believe educators need to advocate for.

But until we have such a system, the tests we now have hold powerful consequences for the futures of educators, schools, and most important, children. They are gates through which all must pass. This is especially true in settings that serve underresourced communities, where public education is one of the few pathways to gain access to a better life. So until accountability policies are changed for the better, educators of conscience in public schools must find a way to balance what seems like two contradictory challenges: On the one hand, we must work to educate people about the limitations of tests, to eliminate punitive policies, and to create more useful assessments; on the other, we must do our best to prepare children to be strong thinkers and learners who can deal with whatever assessment challenges we face.

There are plentiful examples of schools that are able to achieve high scores on standardized tests. In wealthy communities such schools are common. In fact, it has been said that a student's zip code is the best predictor of how he or she will perform on tests. Generally, the more resources the population has, the higher the test scores of its students

(Cassie, 2006; Society for Research in Child Development, 2008). And while the curricula of these schools are constrained by the tests, they generally manage to maintain more enriched curricula and resources than their neighbors in underresourced communities.

In the less common instances where there are high-scoring schools that serve children from low-income communities, especially those with large percentages of children from diverse backgrounds, the high scores are frequently obtained by sacrificing the curriculum to test prep activities (Moon, Callahan, & Tomlinson, 2003). I have seen and read and heard too many stories of such schools that do test practice throughout the entire school year for several hours of each day; where the curriculum mimics not only the content but the format of the tests; where teachers are required to teach through a script that is paced so that everyone is on the same page on the same day; where skills are presented in isolation of meaningful contexts and any hope of getting children to understand is abandoned if they do not grasp the content in the time allotted by the pacing schedule (Jennings & Rentner, 2006; Nichols, Glass, & Berliner, 2005).

In many schools this approach is used not only in the upper test-taking grades but also in classrooms serving the youngest children. More and more, pressures from standardized testing have led not only to standardized teaching but also to a narrow focus on academics at earlier and earlier ages. Worksheets and test preparation are replacing the active learning experiences known to be supportive of young children's learning (Bowman, Donovan, & Burns, 2001; Bredekamp & Copple, 1997). Open-ended activities and imaginative play are all but disappearing in early childhood classrooms. In the quest to prepare younger and younger children for tests, it seems that a good deal of the profession has forgotten how critical it is to support young children's social/emotional as well as cognitive development (Carr, 2004; Elkind, 2001; Gao, 2005; MacDonald, 2005; Zernike, 2000).

My own school-based experiences, as well as my studies of the practices of others who work in urban schools serving diverse populations, demonstrate that teaching the way children learn does not have to be abandoned in the quest for needed content and skills. The curriculum does not have to become test preparation in order for children to perform decently on tests. In fact, when children are immersed in rich learning environments that teach in the ways that they learn, they generally master the skills and knowledge needed for tests in the course of becoming, most important, strong readers, writers, mathematicians, and thinkers (Bredekamp & Copple, 1997; Calkins, Santman, Montgomery, & Falk, 1998).

This has been the case at the Bronx New School. In this book I describe how it has happened. I share stories of how educators teach children from diverse backgrounds to meet the challenging expectations of today's standards without sacrificing support for children's developmental needs or their diverse ways of learning.

Much of what I discuss is about the implementation of developmental theories, pedagogical understandings, and educational reform strategies that are not new. But while research has been done, standards have been developed, reform reports have been written, and educational practices have been altered in efforts to improve schools and schooling, I believe that still more needs to be done. There are not enough descriptions of classrooms and of schools—especially those that serve diverse learners in urban settings—to reveal the invisible inner landscapes of effective work and get beneath the surface of reform buzzwords so that the subtleties that give them meaning can be teased out.

In the pages that follow I offer my efforts to fill in this gap. Part I provides a history and context of the Bronx New School and the ideas that led to its founding. Part II depicts different aspects of teaching that support the way children learn. Part III describes school structures and processes that enable children, their families, and their teachers to be powerful learners and use their minds well. Throughout all that is written I have tried to do justice to the children, educators, and parents represented. While the particularities are unique to this one school and each image of teaching is unique to each teacher, I share them not to offer a cookie-cutter formula for what constitutes good schooling, but rather to present a sense of how shared values and understandings about teaching and about schools' critical role in realizing human potential can both free teachers to teach in their own distinctive manner as well as provide coherence throughout a school.

It has been my experience that when people set out to create new things, unless they are exposed to new models and information, they often unwittingly reproduce variations of what already exists. I hope that what I have written in this book exposes readers to new "images of possibility" and helps to envision how schools can teach in the ways children learn, support them to become powerful thinkers, and celebrate their diversity to enhance their life chances.

PART I

OF HISTORIES
AND CONTEXTS

CHAPTER 1

A School's Beginnings

Before I share images of teaching that supports the learning of many different kinds of children, I provide in this chapter a bit of history about the Bronx New School—its origins, the struggles of its early years, and what has happened to it over time. Good teaching cannot be accomplished in isolation. It requires a community of support. This is the story of how that support began.

PERSONAL PRELUDE

Out of a strong conviction that good pubic schools are essential to the sustenance of our democracy, my family was determined not to send our children to private school and not to flee the richness of New York City's diversity in favor of the more homogeneous suburbs. We committed ourselves to staying in our quiet Bronx neighborhood to try to help make it a better place.

When my daughter Luba entered elementary school, I became active in the parents association in the hopes of contributing through my participation. Through my working with other like-minded parents, small improvements were accomplished. But these had mostly to do with securing enrichment activities for the school, not changing the way teaching and learning was conducted. (The time period was the early 1980s. Understandings about the active nature of young children's learning and the need to teach to the "whole child" were only nascent ideas in public education, considered to be valid not much beyond kindergarten.) So when my neighbors and I raised concerns about the child-unfriendly atmosphere of the school and the routinized teaching in the classrooms, they were not particularly welcomed—by either the professionals or other parents. From what we could tell, the majority of parents involved in school affairs (which we soon found out were only a tiny fraction of the school's families) were not dissatisfied with the teaching and atmosphere of the school. Their children were among those who were doing well, which made sense as we also became aware of the school's unspoken culture that favored the children of activist parents; they seemed to receive a disproportionate distribution of the resources and enrichment activities. Nevertheless, we continued to struggle to find a way to get meaningfully involved and to make some kind of significant change in the quality of learning for all the children in the school.

Meanwhile, Luba was moving up through the grades. Some years were better than others for her, mostly depending on the teacher she had. A few were kind and loving; a few were *not*. Teaching methods varied widely—from old-fashioned strictness to warmth and caring, from copying from the chalkboard to doing creative writing. Because the quality of school life for each child was so dependent on the quality of the classroom teacher, every spring when it came time to decide class configurations for the upcoming year, there would be a buzz among the parents about who was the "best" teacher for the next grade. This would be followed by intense lobbying with the principal from parents "in the know" to get their children into that teacher's class. As much as I wanted my child to have a good teacher, I was really bothered by these maneuvers. I was bothered because I worried about all the children who didn't end up in that "good teacher's" class. I knew that some might get a brand-new teacher who, for lack of experience, might have a rocky time. Or that others might get a teacher who, although seasoned by many years of experience, was stuck in outmoded practices, could easily lose her temper, or had little energy to devote to her teaching. For my own child, however, no matter what happened—whether she ended up with a teacher who was strong or weak—I was still discontented with the overall educational practices and atmosphere of the school.

Disturbing events began to build up. Among them was what Luba and I have come to refer to as "the first-grade notebook incident." I learned of it one night when Luba couldn't sleep, soon after she began first grade. After tossing and turning for what seemed like hours, she burst into tears as she recounted how that morning her teacher had taken her composition notebook away from her. The incident began when Luba, impatient with the slow pace of the teacher's whole-class instructions about how to paste an envelope to the inside covers of the children's notebooks, moved ahead of the explanation to do it by herself. As a result of this maverick act, Luba inadvertently pasted the envelope on the inside *back* cover instead of the inside *front* cover of the notebook. Upon discovering this, the teacher snatched the notebook from Luba's hands and threw it in the garbage, informing Luba that her mother would have to buy her a new notebook so that she could paste the envelope in correctly.

There were many other incidents of teacher rigidity or insensitivity, but I shall recount only a few more. One took place in the third grade, when Luba started getting math problems marked as wrong. Her dad and I couldn't understand why, because all her computations were correct. After investigating the situation we found out that she had copied the problems incorrectly from the chalkboard (part of the assignment—what a waste of time!) because she couldn't see and needed glasses! Luba's teacher never questioned her about this or mentioned to us that there might be something amiss.

But the last straw for us came in the fourth grade, when the teacher informed us that she suspected Luba had lost a spelling bee on purpose because she didn't want the other kids to resent her. It was at that point that Luba's dad and I felt we had no other choice but to move her to a different school. Several of her friends had already transferred to other places.

Meanwhile, our younger daughter, Meryl, was approaching kindergarten age and we knew that we just didn't want to have these same kinds of experiences happen to her. By this time, a small group of neighborhood families had identified a set of "alternative" (before there were such entities as charter schools) public schools in East Harlem—the now-famous Central Park East Schools started by the renowned educator Deborah Meier—that had child-friendly atmospheres and classrooms in which active, project-based learning took place. These families had hired a van (at their own expense) to transport their children there. Although the ride was long, making it necessary for the kids to leave the house before 7:00 A.M., the prospect of having a caring school community that taught children in ways more in tune with how they learn was enticing enough that we soon had Meryl join the daily pilgrimage.

A MOVEMENT IS BORN

As much as I was pleased to have found a school that matched what I wanted for my child, I wanted such a place for my whole neighborhood too. It seemed to me that every community should have a choice of different kinds of schooling that fit their children's and family's needs. So I joined with a group of neighborhood parents and teachers to propose such a school for our local district. What we wanted was a school that had a consistent educational philosophy throughout the grades; that provided children with interesting and active learning experiences; that valued diversity of children's backgrounds as well as learning styles; that offered equitable resources and enrichment to all members of the community;

and that treated parents, teachers, and children as respected partners in the making of their educational choices.

The families involved with the proposal were a diverse group. They came to the project for various reasons. Some, like myself, came from the district's more resource-rich communities where, although in decent physical facilities, they were dissatisfied with the quality of their children's education. They objected to their schools' joyless atmospheres, emphases on rote learning, punitive discipline, and tracking of children into classes that ended up segregating them by race and economic background.

Others came from low-income neighborhoods, where school buildings were crumbling and problems of drugs, crime, and lack of resources were abundant. These families were concerned that their children were not receiving adequate services, that the quality of their education was inferior to that of their counterparts in more affluent sections of the school district, and that their schools' administrations did not welcome their involvement in their children's education.

The two groups met together to work out a mutually acceptable proposal that embraced each group's concerns. Together we crafted a plan for a new "school of choice" that would be open to any interested family in our district. It was to be structured in a way that mixed children from different backgrounds, was to be small enough so that everyone was well known, and would be fashioned into a community that welcomed the involvement of all families. Teaching practices were to be based on the notion that learning is an active and social process, with lots of opportunities for learning by doing, interdisciplinary projects, and the pursuit of understandings in ways that matched children's different learning styles.

We presented our proposal to the school board one summer evening, at a meeting packed by parents from all parts of our district. Stunned by the newfound unity of parents from different neighborhoods as well as different ethnic and socioeconomic backgrounds whose efforts to improve the schools prior to this time had been in isolation and at times, even at odds with each other, the board members, notorious for their own ethnic hostilities and their use of political influence, approved the creation of a new school. We named it the Bronx New School/la Escuela Nueva del Bronx, inspired by a quote from Jose Martí, "El mundo nuevo requiere la escuela nueva," meaning "The new world requires a new kind of school."

LA ESCUELA NUEVA DEL BRONX: BEGINNINGS

Always intended to be small (about 250 students), at least compared with the average New York City public school, the Bronx New School

had a beginning that was even smaller. Since there was no school building available to house a new school, because we were in what was then
one of the most overcrowded districts in New York City, the school was
assigned to operate out of five cramped classrooms in the basement
Sunday School corridor of a local church until a larger space could be
found. Students were selected through a lottery intended to ensure
racial and gender balance (one third Black, Latino and other; one half
boys and one half girls). As a result of massive multilingual outreach
aimed at every corner of the huge district, the school attracted families
from a diverse mix of backgrounds. Three hundred applications were
received to fill the original 75 spots. Seventeen of the 23 schools in
the district were represented. I, who was an experienced school leader
but had never been employed by the New York City public school system, was chosen from more than 70 applicants to become the school's
teacher-director. Since there was no structure in the system at that
time to accommodate small, independent, "alternative" schools, I was
hired on a teacher "line" and we were annexed administratively to another elementary school. Although the principal of that school was our
administrator of record, I reported directly to the superintendent, an
arrangement that was unprecedented in the district and that ruffled
the feathers of many, including that principal. The plan was for the
arrangement to be only temporary; as soon as possible we were to seek
"official" status as our own school and for the director to go through the
official process to become our new school's principal.

The teachers of the school were a mix—ethnically, racially,
experience-wise, and by gender. The unifying element was that all were
enthusiastic supporters of the school's philosophy, which featured close
collaboration between school and family, interage grouping, and classes
that didn't separate children by academic ability. Teaching emphasized
depth rather than superficial coverage of ideas. Children worked collectively as well as individually. The curriculum was designed to build
on their interests while also consciously working to align to standards.
Classrooms were alive with activity—there was hands-on use of materials and lots of creative writing and art. We were among the pioneers
taking a holistic approach to literacy learning, using children's literature rather than textbooks to support classroom learning, applying constructivist learning theory to the teaching of math. We also pioneered
the position of parent coordinator, before New York City school districts
began making them a figure in every school, as well as a part-time
curriculum specialist (this was before schools had literacy and math
coaches), whose job was to help teachers differentiate the curriculum
and be responsive to the diverse ways children learn. The extra personnel needed for these positions were paid for by a small grant solicited

from a private foundation. Everything else was funded through the same per pupil expenditure as that of other schools.

The first 3 years of the school were an exhilarating mix of triumphs and errors. At the beginning there were lots of bureaucratic problems: getting supplies, provisioning the space, working out schedules and routines, dealing with the details of busing and lunches, establishing a working relationship with the "principal of record" and the district administration. There were lots of internal struggles too—about teaching methods, curriculum, discipline, and the appropriate division of labor between parents and professional staff (although everyone always agreed about the importance of each having a say in the school).

As the director, I wrote weekly newsletters to families, featuring articles about all aspects of school life—from explanations of how reading and math were taught, to discussions of problems on the school bus, to reflections on what it means to prepare children for citizenship in a democracy. The teachers regularly sent home curriculum letters, detailing the studies taking place in their classrooms and offering advice on how families could support their children's learning. A weekly all-school meeting devoted to conversation and song helped to develop a sense of community between children, teachers, and the staff. Community was also built through a variety of school structures that involved families: school/family conferences that reviewed children's progress, parent meetings that addressed the philosophy and teaching practices of the school, "celebrations" and "museums"—for sharing the learning that went on in classrooms with other classes and the children's families. In addition, a schoolwide system of assessment and accountability was developed—using performance tasks, teachers' observations, and samples of children's work—to reflect to families and the outside world the full range of learning occurring in the school. This information was also used to inform and shape the instructional program.

The Bronx New School quickly became recognized for its innovative teaching and ways of operating. Despite the school's emphasis on learning rather than testing, students' scores on state tests were impressive. But more important, students were developing a grasp of skills that standardized tests could not reveal: They were thinking deeply, asking provocative questions, grappling with ethical and moral issues, demonstrating compassion for one another, and feeling good about themselves. Some referred to us as a model of school reform and school-based management (Meier, 1991). We were accepted into the alternative school network of the Center for Collaborative Education, the New York City affiliate of the Coalition of Essential Schools. Studied by the National Center for Restructuring Education, Schools, and Teaching (NCREST) at Teachers College, Columbia University, we also participated in an accountability project led by the Educational Testing Service (ETS). Teacher education schools flocked to us with their student teachers. Members of our school community were frequently invited to speak at conferences. We were written about regularly in the local, citywide, and national press.

Almost immediately after the school's beginnings a search for a new larger building began. Although the New York City School Construction Authority was technically responsible for the funding and development of the new site, a committee of parents actually found the building that was to become our permanent home and worked with the Construction Authority to prepare it. One of the school's parents, an architect, designed the structure—in consultation with the staff, the children, their families, and city administrators—so that it would support the school's philosophy and practice. He and the parent-led Site Committee monitored every subsequent step needed for the new school to be built, from the landlord's leasing agreement, to the working drawings based on the original plans, to the construction process, and finally to the certificate of occupancy.

POLITICAL CRISES

After 3 years of growing pains, the school community was coalescing. Educational practices were developing coherence, organizational structures and processes were getting institutionalized, and student performance was remarkably strong. The new site was scheduled to open in the fall of the 4th year. In the meantime, however, a new school board, riding on a backlash against the recent reforms, was elected. They ousted the superintendent who had been responsible for supporting the Bronx New School's creation. In his place they hired a superintendent with a "back to basics" view of teaching who, under the guise of upcoming budget cuts and a controversy in the administrator's union over whether teacher-directors should be allowed to lead schools, began actions to eliminate the school. His plan was to merge the Bronx New School's classrooms with the site to which we had officially been annexed. My position as teacher-director was to be eliminated.

The new superintendent said that the Bronx New School was too autonomous, that its efforts to maintain racial balance and its insistence on independence made it "elitist" and too much like a private school. He and his allies on the school board also charged that the school's rich library of books and learning materials (purchased through Board of Education money we had saved by not buying expensive textbooks), its grant-funded resources (sought out because, given our small size, the school was not entitled to services that were standard in other larger schools) were unfair because these provided for a lucky few a quality education that remained inaccessible to the vast majority of children in the district. Our response to these actions at that time was reflected by what Deborah Meier wrote in an article defending the school: "That's like attacking a low-income housing project because it hasn't solved the housing problems of all low-income people" (1991, p. 338).

Immediately after taking office, only a few weeks before the move to the new building, the new superintendent eliminated my teacher-director position, instructing the principal of the school to which we had been annexed to take over. She, in turn, proceeded to dismantle many of the structures and educational practices we had so painstakingly put into place over the previous years.

THE COMMUNITY RESISTS

Immediately, parents and teachers jumped into action. They and the children wrote letters to local newspapers, testified at school board meetings, held peaceful protest marches, contacted the news media (a defense of the school and my position as director even appeared on the editorial page of the *New York Times* [*New York Times*, 1991]), and initiated a campaign of support for the school that resulted in a flood of letters—from ordinary citizens, local politicians, and national educational figures—to the superintendent, the school board, and the chancellor of the New York City public schools.

What was most moving to me about these reactions was how eloquently the children and their parents spoke about the benefits of the school's philosophy and practice, how deeply they felt ownership of the school, and how passionately they cared about what happened. The following testimony at a public school board meeting given by one of the school's fifth graders exemplifies the community's response:

There are many wonderful things about the Bronx New School.

Instead of black children having their own schools, the Hispanics theirs, the whites theirs, the Bronx New School has all those groups together in one school. This is good because the children can make more friends and they can learn to feel for and understand each other.

Another strength is that if a child at the Bronx New School is having trouble on an assignment, his or her teacher doesn't just yell at them for not understanding the work, that teacher goes over each step with that child and gives that child all the attention that he or she needs until that child understands. Of course, the teachers don't have to, but they do it anyway. And it really helps the students.

At the Bronx New School the children do architecture, learn about electricity and ecology and about how to help the poor of the world and our city. The children learn how to write to our mayor about problems they care about.

In the other school I went to all the children did was learn how to take tests. Once they finished a day's work, the next day they forgot what they had memorized. But at the Bronx New School the children keep the ideas and facts in their heads. And they feel good about that.

In my old school we had to sit in rows of desk and crane our necks to see the teacher and the chalkboard. We never discussed things as a group. All we did all day was sit quietly at our desks and work. At the Bronx New School we don't sit at desks; we sit in a circle and talk with the group.

We don't work in workbooks; we work in our minds. We write about what *we* think, not what the teacher tells us to think. We use different hands-on materials to help us with our work instead of just pencil and paper. Instead of just reading a book and wanting to get finished with it, we the children of the Bronx New School, imagine that we're in that scene in the book and we don't want to finish it. This allows us to have imagination and creativity in our work, which other children in other schools may never get to have.

I am very upset that the Bronx New School has to be destroyed by the School Board.

Despite the efforts to save the school, the superintendent and the school board would not budge in their decision. So the parents took the struggle to another level: They filed a lawsuit against the district (with pro bono assistance from lawyers—one of whom was a school parent) over the right of the Bronx New School families to have input into decisions about their school and the hiring of their leader. The suit went to the New York State Supreme Court, which, after deliberation, ordered the superintendent and school board president to appear before the court to justify their actions.

Only then did the New York City schools chancellor step in to try to help settle the dispute. The chancellor's office worked out a formal agreement that detailed the preservation of the Bronx New School's autonomy in its organizational structure, admissions policies, educational philosophy, and parent involvement. To reach this agreement, however, a compromise had to be made: The parents had to accept the superintendent's decision to have the school supervised by the principal of the school to which we were officially annexed until the end of the school year, at which time the parents would be allowed to vote on how the arrangement was working and whether they felt it was satisfactory. If they determined that it wasn't—which was what eventually happened—the Bronx New School community would be given official status as a separate school and allowed to select the school's leader.

A VICTORY—OF SORTS

Although this settlement meant that I could no longer remain as the director of the school, we all agreed that it was a victory because the right of the school to exist had been won. Happy for the school but personally heartbroken, I officially stepped aside. The school year, which had got off to a rocky start, continued that way through the ensuing months. In June, as predicted, the parents voted out the principal chosen by the superintendent and the school was awarded official status as its own "school." A new principal was selected with active input from the school community. (Although I had a principal's license, I did not seek the position, as I had begun to pick up the pieces of my own life and had moved on to get involved with other work.) Meanwhile, another school board election had taken place, resulting in still another dramatic shift in politics. (Several members of the old board were forced to leave because they had been indicted for alleged election fraud.) The new board selected a new superintendent who now heralded the Bronx New School as a model for the district and began creating other small schools featuring many of the elements of child-centered teaching that the Bronx New School had pioneered.

LESSONS LEARNED

One of the big lessons I learned from all that happened is that if a school has clear values, explains them well, and involves all members of the community in its work, the values will get embedded in its "walls" and endure despite hardship and leadership changes. This is what happened with the Bronx New School. It survived the crises of its early years. Over the years it has weathered still other crises and gone through many other transformations—another change in the principal, staff comings and goings, modifications to the grade configurations, and negotiations with the curriculum to comply with the ever-fluctuating policies and mandates of public education.

But in spite of all this, the founding values of the school remain intact today. It is still a multiethnic, multicultural school of choice committed to the child-centered vision and practices of its founders. Overcoming top-down mandates and high-stakes testing pressures from the world beyond the school, students continue to perform well on standardized tests without teachers surrendering the curriculum to test prep. Active learning, integrated studies, attention to the social/emotional aspects of children's development, and an emphasis on the arts continue to be the school's signature qualities. It stands as an example of the changes that are possible when teachers, parents, and community come together around a shared vision and purpose for education.

I tell this saga of how the Bronx New School survived because what happened to it, unfortunately, is not so uncommon in the highly politicized atmosphere that seems to characterize public education. It is a story that reveals many of the complex factors that affect schools and their futures. And it demonstrates that, despite the influence of these factors, it is possible not only to survive, but also to endure. Over the years, the Bronx New School has done just that.

And although, just as in its founding years, the Bronx New School today still struggles both outwardly and inwardly—with the politics and structures of the system as well as among the members of its school community about the particularities of its operations—it is precisely these kinds of ongoing struggles that make this school (and the ever-growing cadre of small schools that are like it) so special. These kinds of schools are special because they consciously become a community—of teachers, parents, and children alike—made of people who exercise their intelligence on a daily basis and actually find joy in the process. As such, schools like the Bronx New School offer hope to all of us who believe that public education is vital to democracy. They are testimony to the fact that public schools have the capacity to be imaginative, exciting, and supportive places that are able to educate children well.

In the chapters that follow I reference stories from the Bronx New School, from the founding as well as recent period, to describe some of the central practices and qualities that characterize effective child-centered learning environments that serve diverse learners in urban schools. I also share my recollections and current reflections about the ongoing challenges that face educators who are committed to doing this kind of work. But first, I discuss the larger context of ideas and understandings upon which these practices have been built.

CHAPTER 2

Contexts: The Evolution of Child-Centered Thinking and Teaching

The ideas and practices of the Bronx New School have a long history rooted in the research, values, and purposes of child-centered education. This chapter traces the evolution of these ideas and their implications for schooling.

Child-centered schools in the Western world are philosophically rooted in the work of educators and philosophers of the 18th and early 19th centuries (Jean-Jacques Rousseau, 1712–1778; Johann Heinrich Pestalozzi, 1746–1827; and Friedrich Froebel, 1782–1852) who believed that schools should be observant of children's interests and responsive to their needs. These individuals were convinced, as were those who built on their ideas after them, that the purpose of education was to create the conditions for children's development and autonomy while establishing a pattern of support for each child's continuous progress within a school community nurtured by a democratic ethic (Dewey, 1916, 1938, 1956). Their ideas were enriched and expanded on over the years through the work of many other educators, researchers, and philosophers.

ROOTS

"Child-centered" thinking can be traced to the ideas of John-Jacques Rousseau, a Swiss philosopher, author, and social reformer who lived in the 18th century. In his book *Emile*, he set forth the notion that education should nurture a child's natural capabilities. Education, said Rousseau, should begin not where some adult has decided is appropriate, but where the child begins (Rousseau, 1762).

Prior to Rousseau, ideas about children were based on the belief that they were simply deficient adults. Children were seen as lacking knowledge, self-discipline, and purpose. The task of education was viewed as instilling these qualities in them. As a result, schools were grim and punitive places. Proverbs and scriptures were used to teach basic skills. Thought was simply not given to developing materials or methods that would be naturally interesting (Farnham-Diggory, 1990).

It took until the late 18th century for a school to be established that embodied Rousseau's ideas. Started by a disciple, Johann Heinrich Pestalozzi, this school was followed in the early 19th century with one created by another of Rousseau's disciples, Friedrich Froebel, who later became known as the originator of kindergartens. Later, followers of these educators—Francis Parker in North America, the McMillan sisters in England, Maria Montessori in Italy—began schools for children that embraced one or another of their principles (Feeney, Christensen, & Moravcik, 2005). Thus began a movement of education that honored children's individual needs and differences; that recognized the importance of motivation and interest in learning; that promoted active learning over rote memorization; that developed curricula integrating the disciplines, and that took into account each child's total social, physical, intellectual, and emotional development.

JOHN DEWEY AND THE PROGRESSIVES

These ideas were developed further by John Dewey, an American philosopher who established the Chicago Lab School in the early 20th century to test out his beliefs about human learning and community. Weaving together the thoughts and practices of Rousseau, Pestalozzi and Froebel, Dewey's school was built upon the notions that education and life are interconnected, not separate pieces; that experience is the basis for all learning; that the interests of the learner must guide curriculum development; and that the development of intelligence and knowledge is dependent on social interaction (Dewey, 1916, 1938, 1956).

Dewey's influence extended to others whose work was in different disciplines, most notably the Child Study Movement in psychology, first led by G. Stanley Hall, which focused on learning about human behavior by observing children. The ideas developed out of this movement became the basis of what has since become known as progressive education, named thus originally because it was an education that followed the "progress" of the child. Among those it influenced were Harriet Johnson, Patty Smith Hill, Lucy Sprague Mitchell, Caroline Pratt—pioneers in the field of North American early childhood education—who were responsible for establishing such important organizations as the Bank Street School for Children, the National

Association for the Education of Young Children, and later, the federally supported early learning initiative that came to be known as Head Start (Greenberg, 1987).

Many subsequent school reform initiatives, most notably the open education movement of the 1960s and 1970s and the small-schools movement launched in the 1980s, which continues to this day, are also built on the ideals of progressive education. Influential was the Open Corridor initiative in the New York City public schools that was led in the late 1960s by Lillian Weber, the founder of The City College Workshop Center Advisory. This initiative was committed to enacting teaching practices and organizational structures in public school settings that reflected understandings of how children learn. Working with teachers of elementary-grade classrooms who shared a corridor in selected New York City public schools, Weber and a cadre of colleagues helped them "open" up their classrooms to encourage active inquiry-based learning experiences that freed children from the confinement of desks and paper-and-pencil tasks, used the hallways as centers for learning, and mixed children of different abilities and ages. The teaching and learning that took place in these corridors raised awareness of the many different kinds of contexts and resources that can nurture children's growth.

The practices developed in these corridors were also instrumental in stimulating thinking about how to apply understandings of teaching and learning not only to children, but also to the adults who were responsible for their care. Weber's colleagues acted as corridor advisors to assist in this process. They were experienced teachers themselves who were knowledgeable about child development, were sensitized to issues of adult learning, and possessed a range of teaching strategies supportive of both teachers' and students' learning. They worked one day a week in each corridor program, always independent of the supervisory structure, providing teachers with continual opportunities to discuss and get feedback on their practice. They helped to support teachers to connect to their own interests, engage in their own inquiry, experience themselves as learners, and break with the traditional isolation of teachers and children in their own classrooms (Weber, 1991).

This pioneering work was in large part responsible for the emergence of a new view of the teacher's role and a new conceptualization of the nature of professional development. The teacher's role was being crafted as that of a facilitator of student learning rather than simply a transmitter of information. Conceptions of professional development were changing from a deficit to a capacity-building model—making a shift from "training" teachers in the use of teaching packages and recipes to developing and supporting teachers' varied strengths in the same way teachers were being asked to support children (Lieberman & Falk, 2007).

During the same period in which the Open Corridor initiative was launched, a national test-driven "back to basics" movement, emphasizing mastery of basic skills as a prerequisite for higher-order thinking, was competing with the Corridor's emphasis on developing habits of ongoing student inquiry. This was reflected in a proliferation of teacher-proof, sequential, discipline-based curricula that were discouraging efforts to get teachers to create their own multidimensional, interdisciplinary studies.

Despite the setbacks to child-centered education caused by this clash with the back-to-basics movement, many of the practices that were being forged by Weber and her colleagues have since become commonly acknowledged as meeting high standards of excellence in contemporary professional practice. Classrooms featuring informal arrangements, active involvement with materials and experiences, an inquiry-based orientation, interage and heterogeneous grouping, and authentic assessment of student work are increasingly accepted today as an integral part of the movement for educational reform (Darling-Hammond, 1997).

CONSTRUCTIVIST AND
SOCIAL CONSTRUCTIVIST THEORIES

More theories and studies of learning over the years lend support to the early theories and practices underpinning child-centered education.

Through his observational studies of infants and young children, Jean Piaget, a Swiss psychologist, first developed new understandings about how people learn. As a result he described learning as a process of building cognitive structures through active and social interactions that build on prior knowledge and experiences (Piaget, 1973, 1975, 1998, 2000; Piaget & Inhelder, 1969). After Piaget, others studied how young children integrate sight and sound and explore their perceptual worlds (Gibson, 1969; Newell, Shaw, & Simon, 1958). Although these theories differ in important ways, they share an emphasis on seeing children as active learners who are able to set goals, to plan, and to revise.

This active role that children play in their own learning was also emphasized by Lev Vygotsky (1978), a Russian psychologist who pointed out how people and the social environment influence the development of each child's thinking. He theorized that each person has a *zone of proximal development* that learners can navigate with assistance from others or from a supportive context (Vygotsky, 1978). His ideas were developed further by others, who emphasized the impact that family, community, and culture have (through both formal and informal teaching) on children's efforts to understand the world (Brown & Reeve, 1987; Lave & Wenger, 1991; Moll & Whitmore, 1993; Newman, Griffin, & Cole, 1989; Rogoff & Wertsch, 1984). The work of these researchers support the theories of educational philosophers who emphasize that all human beings have a deep drive to make sense out of the world (Bruner, 1966; Carini, 1987); that learning is something a learner does, not something that is done to a learner.

BEHAVIORAL THEORIES: AN OPPOSING VIEW

The idea that learners construct understandings by connecting new information to their own prior knowledge and experience presents itself in opposition to the notion, long dominant in Western education, that the learner is an empty vessel in need of filling up. It also contrasts with behavioral theories of learning, which conceptualize learning as the transmittal of facts and skills. Behavioral theories emerged from the field of psychology's experimental studies of animals. Since behavioral psychologists found that a stimulus followed with reinforcement could get rats and other animals to perform specified behaviors on command, they reasoned that humans functioned in similar ways. They thus conceptualized learning as an incremental process of mastering increasingly complex skills. Logically, this resulted in their advocacy of teaching methods that emphasize practice and repetition of skills reinforced by punishments or rewards (Skinner, 1954).

Behaviorism still heavily influences psychology as well as teaching today. The programmed instruction found in many basal readers, workbooks, and curricular materials is based on behavioral theory. Tests' heavy reliance on short-answer, fill-in-the-blank, or multiple-choice formats also stems from a behavioral stance. Because behaviorist perspectives view learning as primarily skill mastery and the accumulation of individual bits of knowledge, it follows, from this point of view, that short-answer, fill-in-the-blank, or multiple-choice questions can effectively evaluate if learning has indeed taken place.

The influence of behaviorism on education is not confined only to teaching methods, however. It affects school curricula and accountability structures too. It is seen in the "direct instruction" curricula used in many classrooms and in the standardized curricula mandated in many schools. It is the driving force behind "high stakes" consequences associated with test performance. Based on the belief that control and extrinsic rewards are the motivators for what people do, behavioral theories negate the notion of intrinsic motivation that stimulates and harnesses learning. Behavioral theories are what underpin the idea that learning and behavior outcomes can best be shaped through sanctions and rewards. They influence the top-down bureaucratic structures and policies that are in place in many school districts around this country.

REFUTATION: CONTRIBUTIONS FROM NEUROSCIENCE

Recent evidence emerging from cognitive science and neuroscience suggests that the standardized teaching, testing, and schooling rooted in behaviorist conceptions of learning actually get in the way of creating environments supportive of the learning needs of diverse students. Through neuroimaging technologies developed in the past few decades, scientists have actually been able to observe how neural connections are made. This information has enabled them to confirm that the human organism is literally wired to learn; that individuals actively participate in their own growth; that the development and collaboration of various processing systems in the brain—indeed, the actual architecture of the brain—starts at birth and continues at an explosive rate, enhanced by active engagement with materials, ideas, and relationships. It is in this way that individuals learn. New information, concepts, and ideas are integrated with the brain structures formed from past experiences to realize new skills, understandings, and knowledge (Bowman, Donovan, & Burns, 2001; Bransford, Brown, & Cocking, 2000; Shonkoff & Phillips, 2000).

Neuroimaging technologies have also demonstrated how affective aspects of people's lives—such as the presence of relevance, interest, enjoyment, good relationships, feelings of safety, and self-efficacy—are important supporters of learning, while pointing to how stress, boredom, confusion, low motivation, and anxiety interfere with the process (Viadero, 2007; Willis, 2007). Without a doubt, the cognitive and emotional aspects of development are intricately intertwined.

Other research has led to additional understandings about a link between cognitive and social development. Children's social relationships and their social environment—specifically the family, community and culture—have been found to have an important impact (through both formal and informal teaching) on children's efforts to understand the world (Bowman et al., 2001; Rogoff, 2003). This includes language and culture, too, which also profoundly affect children's learning (Au & Jordan, 1981; Ballenger, 1998; Banks, 2006; Cummins, 2001; Krashen, 1996; Ladson-Billings, 1994, 2005).

Furthermore, the research is clear that learning is not just a cognitive and physical process but also a social and emotional phenomenon. Emotions and social relations influence all aspects of cognitive growth. The ways that children live their lives become interwoven in the brain (Siegel, 2001). In other words, whether or not children live in supportive environments of caring adults in families, schools, neighborhoods, communities, and our larger society makes a difference to their development (Brown & Campione, 1996; Rogoff, 2003; Sampson, Sharkey, & Raudenbush, 2007).

Another understanding that the research makes clear is that development does not proceed in a uniform, one-size-fits-all manner. Rather, different children bring different strengths and intelligences to the learning process (Gardner 1983, 1991, 1997). They develop at different paces and in different ways. Diversity and variation are the norm (Bredekamp & Copple, 1997).

These more recent understandings about how people learn have led to widespread recognition of the kind of teaching and teaching environments that are best able to support learning.

TRANSFORMING VIEWS
OF TEACHING AND THE ROLE OF THE TEACHER

Perhaps the biggest area affected by new understandings of learning is how we view teaching and the role of the teacher. Findings from cognitive science and neuroscience research give credence to what Martin Heidegger (cited in Carini, 1987, p. 14) calls "teaching to let learn."

> What does it mean to let learn, to let learning occur? . . . It means a teaching that releases the impulse to learn in the learner. The idea envisions a teaching that, in fashioning itself as a bridge or a path, connects the learner to the world media and to ideas capable of extending and deepening the learner's thought. Teaching that is teaching to let learn enlightens, opens up, and increases the meaning and value of the learner's experience, thought, and ideas. The emphasis in this teaching is on knowledge of what the learner *cares* about and how that *caring* can be supported and extended through ideas and by access to the media and processes through which the learner's interests can find shape and form. (Carini, 1987, p. 14)

This kind of teaching pays attention to the knowledge, skills, attitudes, and beliefs that learners bring to the educational setting. It offers learners opportunities to actively engage with materials, relationships, and experiences to "construct" their knowledge about the world. It is facilitated by teachers who are knowledgeable about the content they teach and who know how to help learners develop deep understandings of that content through meaningful and purposeful activities. Such teachers know how to gather and use a wide range of information about their learners to guide their instruction. They work to build on learners' interests and strengths to support learners' overall development—social, emotional, and physical, as well as cognitive. They are responsive to the different learning styles and "intelligences" of their learners as well as their learners' cultural and linguistic backgrounds. They consciously reach out to make connections between school, family, and community.

In recent years, many of these ideas of teaching have been translated into practice and become more prevalent in mainstream classrooms. Professional associations have also used these ideas to formulate guidelines for the development of curriculum content (American Association for the Advancement of Science, 1993; Association for Supervision and Curriculum Development, 2007; International Reading Association and the National Council of Teachers of English, 1996; National Association for the Education of Young Children and National Association for Early Childhood Specialists in State Departments of Education, 2003; National Council of Teachers of Mathematics, 2000; National Commission on Social Studies in the Schools, 1990; and others).

Teaching methods and educational policies have also been refined based on these ideas. The process approach to reading and writing (Calkins, 1994, 2000; Graves, 2003), project-based work (Katz & Chard, 2000), efforts to teach for understanding (Blythe, 1997; Cohen, McLaughlin, & Talbert, 1993; Wiske, 1997), differentiated curricula responsive to "multiple intelligences" and diverse learners (Delpit, 2002, 2006a, 2006b; Gardner, 1991; Gay, 2000; Ladson-Billings, 2005; Tomlinson, 2004), strategies for teaching to diverse linguistic populations (Cummins, 2001; Krashen, 1996; Krashen, Tse, & McQuillan, 1998), initiatives that build home/school/community partnerships (Comer, Haynes, Joyner, & Ben-Avie, 1999; Epstein, 2002; Zigler, Gilliam, & Jones, 2006), and instruction in mathematics emphasizing problem solving and the meaning behind symbols (Terc, 2006) are now accepted in many schools.

However, these ideas and practices are less prevalent in urban communities that serve children of color and low-income backgrounds. The emphasis in such settings, more often than not, seems to be on learning "basic skills" in preparation for tests. This "basic skills" orientation is a holdover of behaviorist notions that only when students master foundational content and skills can they focus on such "higher order" processes as critical thinking, analysis, and reflection. And since disproportionate numbers of students from low-income urban communities of color lag behind in attaining high test scores, "those children," the logic continues, need to be fed a steady diet of a test prep curriculum at the expense of activities considered to be "extras"—such as trips; hands-on experiences; instruction in science; social studies, and the arts; and, sometimes in the earliest grades, even recess and naptime.

But this logic flies in the face of the evidence that learning—for both children and adults—takes place in contexts that have meaning as well as purpose to the learner; that basic skills develop in the context of work on meaningful, higher-order skills and processes; that it is when children are exposed to the world, talked to a lot, and given opportunities to actively engage in interesting activities that they literally soak up knowledge and understandings. This is precisely what children from well-resourced backgrounds get at home from their family and community experiences before they ever step foot inside a school. And it is what accounts, to a great degree, for their seemingly greater abilities to handle the more abstract instruction to which they are introduced when they are in school.

The "logic" of the skills-based approach to teaching diverse learners in urban communities is rife with still other flaws. The "stripped down" curriculum of skills that are taught in only one way contradicts research-based understandings that learners have different strengths and preferences; that some learn best through one modality while others learn better in another. It doesn't make sense that such a "one-size-fits-all" approach to teaching is so prevalent in situations where it is already known that so many children have not been successful learning in this uniform way on expected outcomes. Wouldn't it make sense, especially in such contexts, to try teaching with a more diverse range of strategies?

One explanation for the discrepancies between how children are taught in diverse urban communities as opposed to more affluent ones can be found in the different perspectives on the purposes of education that drive teaching and learning in schools.

VALUES, ASSUMPTIONS, AND PURPOSES

The kind of future we envision for the children of our society influences the way we educate them. When Horace Mann founded the "common school" in the mid-19th century, his purpose was to ensure that the broad masses of people (of course, at that time it was only White people) acquired basic knowledge and skills. With the emancipation of slaves, industrialization of our economy, compulsory school attendance laws, and waves of immigration during the late 19th and early 20th centuries, the purpose of public education increasingly became "training" the masses of people to achieve the minimal level of literacy and numeracy needed for industrial jobs.

This purpose of education shaped the design and nature of U.S. schools, which began in the farming era as one-room schoolhouses. They were also influenced by Henry Ford's invention of the factory assembly line and Frederick Taylor's (1911) conceptions of scientific management (both of which emanate from the behavioral theory that there is one best way to do every job and this way can be broken down into repetitive tasks that require a specified amount of time).

Thus, the one-room schoolhouses of the farming era were replaced by huge schools. Students were separated into tracks by so-called ability, sequenced from one grade to another, circulated from classroom to classroom, regulated with bell schedules and time clocks, instructed through a series of textbooks, and monitored with standardized tests to efficiently keep track of their learning (Darling-Hammond, 1997). Dubbed "factory model" schools, they reflected not only theories of behavioral psychology but also an economic perspective on the purposes of education: to ensure that one group of people was educated to lead while others (the much larger group) were educated to be followers. Special "tracks" were created to provide an elite group with curricula and learning experiences that would develop the higher-level understandings and skills needed to enhance their capacity to think. The majority, who were to be the followers, received a curriculum aimed only at fostering low-level skills (Tyack, 1974).

This view of the purpose of schooling continues to hold sway over public thinking and investment in education today. Despite the fact that conditions have changed and that factory jobs in this country are being eliminated, there are too many outmoded factory-model schools still operating that are not adequately preparing youth for the skills and knowledge they need to survive in our technological, global economy.

A competing view to the perspective that the purpose of schools is solely economic is the human development perspective first attributed to John Dewey. Grounded in knowledge of how children learn and strong beliefs about the benefits of participatory democracy, this view argues that schools should do more than just prepare citizens for their economic role in society and teach for more than just minimal levels of competency. Rather, it regards the purpose of schools to be to help *all* individuals, not just the elite, learn to think deeply and realize their potential in order to transform themselves and contribute to public democratic life (Dewey, 1916). Such a philosophy has flourished at times over the past 150 years of public education—in the early 1900s; in the 1930s and 1940s; in the late 1960s; and once again in the school reform initiatives begun in the late 1980s, many of which continue to this day. It is a philosophy advocating teaching practices that focus on the holistic development of each learner, that emphasizes understanding and thinking—not just skill drill and rote memorization. It supports as well the establishment of school structures that create a sense of community and provide all with opportunities for democratic participation (Cremin, 1964).

From an ethical and moral perspective, to me, the Deweyan purposes of schooling make sense. While I believe that one part of the responsibility of schooling is to prepare people to economically survive, survival is much more than economic. It also involves nourishing the spirit and developing our overall human capacities so that we can contribute to the discourse and betterment of public life. If we are ever to realize, for all people, the self-actualization goals of democracy, then all children need to have opportunities to experience a rich curriculum that can enhance their life chances and lead them to unlimited possibilities. The complex issues facing our human community require

> the creation of men and women who are capable of doing new things, not simply repeating what others have done—men and women who are creative, inventive and discoverers . . . who can be critical, can verify, and not accept everything they are offered. (Piaget, cited in Greene, 1978, p. 80)

Today and for the future—for the very survival of our planet—we need schools to nurture the skills, knowledge, and dispositions of all learners so that they can imagine new ideas, carry out change, and be truly independent thinkers. To accomplish this, schools need to foster every child's love for learning as well as his or her interest and responsibility in the world. Vito Perrone framed it this way:

> What do we most want our students to come to understand as a result of their schooling? "Reading and writing" might be a quick response, but is this enough? What if our students learn to read and write but don't like to and don't? What if they don't read newspapers and magazines, or can't find beauty in a poem or love story?. . .What if they don't go as adults to artistic events, don't listen to a broad range of music, aren't optimistic about the world and their place in it, don't

notice the trees and the sunset, don't look at the stars, are indifferent to older citizens, don't participate in politics or community life, aren't prepared for the responsibility of parenthood, don't have a vision of themselves as thoughtful mothers and fathers, and are physically and psychologically abusive to themselves? And what if they can locate the Republic of South Africa but don't know anything about apartheid and can't feel the pain associated with it? Know about hunger, and collectively waste tons of food each day? (1991. p. 4)

Such an education needs to be oriented toward a broader range of things than simply the acquisition of knowledge.

There are skills and activities, feelings, and emotions that need to be attended to; there is the sense of community to be fostered, along with the recognition of our solidarity with other living beings; there is the natural context to be heeded and understood. (Noddings, 1984, pp. 56–57)

Throughout history, education has been a catalyst for people to transform themselves and their situations. It has been instrumental in widening horizons, opening perspectives, discovering possibilities, and overcoming obstacles. It has served as a road to empowerment and freedom (Freire, 1971). W.E.B. DuBois saw this purpose as essential for all citizens, calling it "the right to learn":

The right to have examined in our schools not only what we believe, but what we do not believe; not only what our leaders say, but what the leaders of other groups and nations, and the leaders of other centuries have said. We must insist upon this to give our children the fairness of a start which will equip them with such an array of facts and such an attitude toward truth that they can have a real chance to judge what the world is and what its greater minds have thought it might be. (1970, pp. 230–231)

School's responsibility in a democracy is to provide "the right to learn" to all. Everyone should be given "the opportunity and the capacity to reach beyond, to move toward what is not yet" (Greene, 1978, pp. 22–23), to realize his or her hopes and pursue his or her dreams. It is in the context of these values and purposes that the educational practices discussed in the next chapters reside.

PART II

Images of Possibility: Teaching

CHAPTER 3

Morning Meeting: Infusing Skills and Content Knowledge into Real-World Problems and Experiences

Part of what is needed to develop the capacity to realize one's hopes and dreams is a firm grasp of the knowledge and skills demanded and evaluated by local and state standards and tests. Given the proliferation of educational policies that pay or punish teachers, schools, and even students for their performance on these tests, skill development is a big concern in classrooms. This chapter offers images of teaching that builds skills without rote drill. Rather, the approach I describe infuses skills and content knowledge into routines that form the backbone of the class day. Skills are introduced, practiced, and developed through interesting and meaningful activities that not only strengthen children's academic abilities but also nurture their social and emotional development, their dispositions to learn, and ultimately their abilities to engage in the discourse of democracy.

The routines described here are part of the morning meeting of a mixed kindergarten/1st-grade class at the Bronx New School. These routines are not dissimilar to classroom routines at other elementary schools around the country. What is different and of interest about them, however, is the degree to which activities that could easily be perfunctory, even boring, are used as rich opportunities for learning. My description of this small portion of the school day focuses specifically on the way Ronnie (note: names of adults used throughout the book are real; names of children are pseudonyms), an experienced teacher, attended explicitly to skill development in the context of activities that involve children in problem solving and problem posing. As she conducted the morning meeting, Ronnie used what she learned about her students to shape her teaching, celebrate the diversity of each child, and nurture the group to become a community.

Morning meeting in Ronnie's class was a time when the children came together to discuss their ideas, share their experiences, and review the upcoming events of the school day. They reviewed the schedule for their day, took attendance, noted the number of days they had been in school, marked the date on the calendar, took notice of current weather conditions, kept track of who had brought lunch from home and who required school lunch, reminded each other of class jobs, and celebrated each other and their backgrounds by interviewing different children about their lives. Charts documenting the information contained in these routines hung on the classroom walls and were used by the teacher and the children as a resource for the learning that took place during the day (see Figure 3.1).

The meeting was structured to encourage the children's participation and choice. After getting familiar with the routines at the beginning of the school year, everyone in the class was invited each day to volunteer to lead an activity of his or her choosing. This access to choice was deliberately provided because Ronnie understood the importance of choice for building the confidence and sense of agency children need to be active thinkers and learners (Bowman et al., 2001; Bransford et al., 2000; Resnick, 1987).

The meeting usually began with a review of the "flow of the day" chart, a routine that lists the order of the day's activities (see Figure 3.2). This review supported children's learning by giving them a sense of predictability and stability, important preventatives for individual or class discipline problems (Bredekamp & Copple, 1997).

ROUTINES

Taking attendance and making the lunch chart are examples of routines that are rich with opportunities for learning. As the children first entered the classroom in the morning, they stopped at the attendance chart (see Figure 3.3), which has colorful Velcro-backed people figures (each crafted by the child whose it name it bears).

Children each removed their own figure and placed it on either the home lunch or school lunch chart, depending on whether they brought lunch from home or ate school food. (This information was subsequently tallied by the children and delivered by one of them first to the school office to report attendance and then to the lunchroom to assist the food staff in planning the meals for that day.)

The child selected to lead the lunch chart routine sorted and then counted out loud the number of figures on the charts—first the home

FIGURE 3.1. Classroom charts

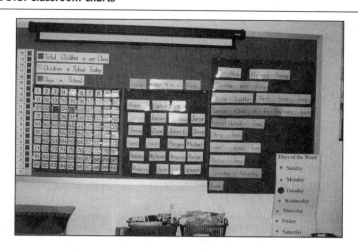

FIGURE 3.2. Flow of the day chart

FIGURE 3.3. Attendance chart (top) and lunch charts (bottom)

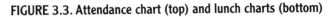

lunches and then the school lunches. Then the child explained to the class how he or she grouped the figures to come up with the final sum. The count was first double checked and then triple checked by different children to ensure the accuracy of the final number. Each child who counted was encouraged to sort the figures in different groupings and to explain to the class why he or she grouped them in this way.

At the beginning of the school year, the children generally counted the people figures one by one. As the days and months progressed, however, they began counting in groups of twos, threes, fours, and fives. By midyear I witnessed one child counting the 15 figures on the school lunch chart as "seven groups of two and one extra." Another sorted the figures and counted "five groups of three." Another came up and used the same sorting but counted them as "two groups of five and five extras." Ronnie repeated back to him what he had just said and then, after waiting a few moments for him to reflect, asked: "Does five extras make a group of five?" This prompt helped him to quickly realize that it did and he modified his answer to pronounce that the chart contained "three groups of five."

From this activity Ronnie explained that

> the children are learning to visualize numbers, verbalize the different ways of their visualizing numbers and how they are putting the numbers together and taking numbers apart. This is what makes somebody have a good, strong number sense. It's interesting to see how certain kids see a two by three array as groups of two, where others can see it as groups of three. Doing things like this gets kids to start seeing things in different ways. And they love it! They want to double check, triple check, quadruple check. So, everything that we use in the morning meeting becomes a reference for their later learning. When they're doing math and I ask, "Well, did you double check?" they see meaning and a reason for it because they've lived the importance of it here. And so it just becomes a habit of the way they think.

As the children learned how to collect data and to understand concepts through their daily routines, the charts they used offered different models and tools to solve problems. By applying these tools to the real-world problems that they experienced every day, the children learned, in meaningful ways, that there are multiple strategies for figuring things out. They also gained flexibility to apply these different strategies to other areas of their learning.

To support the children as they worked with new strategies, Ronnie employed a variety of teaching approaches. She reflected back to children what they said and built on what they already knew (as in her probe about what makes a "group of five" to the child who said he had two groups of five and five extras). She also asked questions that pushed for deeper meaning, insisting that, when offering an answer, they show and explain what they mean. All these teaching methods helped to ensure that the children really understand what they said and did (Cohen, McLaughlin, & Talbert, 1993). Ronnie elaborated:

> I make the link for them to get them thinking along a path if they haven't made the link themselves. Sometimes it's just a little prompt that is needed. "Oh, yeah, right!" That does it.

CRITICAL THINKING

Critical thinking and analysis were emphasized in the morning meeting routines. When filling out the weather chart, for example, the children in the class were polled for their assessment of the day's climate (is it partly cloudy? sunny? or other possibilities?) Whatever the majority decided is what was noted on a weather tally that got counted at the end of each week and month. The purpose of this process was to listen to what the others had to say and to learn how to base conclusions on evidence. Ronnie explained:

> It's not so much about whether it's partly cloudy or sunny, but what are you basing it on? It's really not about the actuality, because weather changes, but rather it is about being able to use evidence. And also it's about learning to listen and being a part of a community. The children have to listen to each other's voices, think about what each other is saying, and then either change or not change their thinking.

BUILDING A COMMUNITY OF LEARNERS

The weather routine, like others in the morning meeting, built a sense of community among the children. As they talked and listened to each other (see Figure 3.4), they developed a feel for what it is like to be an active participant in a group. Ronnie elaborated:

FIGURE 3.4. Meeting with weather chart

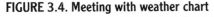

The key thing is to be respectful of one another. So even though you may not understand what Josue is saying right now, let's give him a chance to say it to us and think about what he's going to say. Because maybe he hasn't really figured it out in his own mind yet; so maybe there isn't an answer that day; but there's time and space provided for him to do it and that makes a difference in how we all feel about each other and us as a community and it's sort of the approach all around, the expectation. There are even times when kids cheer for one another 'cause they've seen kids who are trying to do something and then one day—like especially the kindergartners who were only counting by ones and couldn't count by twos for so long—when someone finally did it, everyone just immediately clapped. So it's making that time to be heard. Even if you've not been entirely understood, that's OK too. And that speaks for itself in how the children feel for each other and really are there for one another.

This sense of support and feeling of community in the classroom was nurtured in other ways. One was the routine of "Child of the Day," in which a child is called up at the morning meeting to share his or her background and culture with the entire class. (See Figure 3.5.) Being selected "Child of the Day" is not a reward reserved for good behavior

FIGURE 3.5. Child of the day

or work, but rather an opportunity for the class to learn about and celebrate every child. What the child shares is written down on a chart, providing another opportunity during the many in the day for the class to work on skill development—to learn about sentence structure, new vocabulary words, punctuation, and other conventions of print. Here again is an instance of how skill work is woven into an activity that has a much larger purpose: to honor the diversity of the children, their families, and their backgrounds as valuable resources for learning (Ladson-Billings, 1994; Moll, 1995).

These and other routines during the day not only support children's learning, but also create a sense of community among the children by building norms of interaction. One of these norms is listening to others and exchanging ideas respectfully. Ronnie modeled this because she knew that children learn best when they feel safe and are in a community of support (Boyer, 1995; Noddings, 1992). For example, if children were talking while a child was presenting, she reminded them not to call out by offering them suggestions for what they *should* do, rather than what they should *not* do. In a quiet, calm voice she explained that "Davre is the counter now. Let's give our full attention to Davre," or "Some of you may think you are helping Victor by giving him the answer, but the best way to help him is to give him time to figure things out." This modeling paid off in the caring interactions children exhibited with each other. One notable example I remember is when during a meeting the child leading the calendar routine could not reach the calendar tacked up on the wall when she tried to write down the date on it. Another child, without being prompted, got up from the circle to bring a chair for the first child to stand on so that she could reach it.

Ronnie also modeled respect for different perspectives. She invited children to offer different points of view. Whether it was showing a different strategy for counting, making a judgment about the weather, or expressing an opinion that differed from those of others, each individual was encouraged to contribute.

Additionally, she offered the children continual opportunities for choice by inviting the children to decide each day in which order they would go through their routines. Doing this cultivated children's sense of autonomy and self-efficacy—essentials of healthy, overall development that can powerfully affect learning (Bowman et al., 2001; Bransford et al., 2000; Bredekamp & Copple, 1997). As she explained:

> All the sharing and listening and noticing that we do together, although not obvious to the children, affect the feelings that they carry around with them, which, in turn, affect their abilities to learn.

KNOWING LEARNERS WELL

Teachers need to know their students well for effective learning to take place (Bowman et al., 2001). The routines of the morning meeting are ripe with opportunities for teachers to learn about their students' different understandings, intelligences, and learning styles—information Ronnie used to shape her instruction. She elaborated:

> Everything we do gives me a picture, gives me information that leads me to understand each child better. The meeting is one of the opportunities I have to do a lot of noticing. Sometimes a child will want to lead the same routine day after day. That is very telling for me. I look at what that child's interest or reason for wanting to do that is. Is it something they are working on? Is it the confirmation that they need? Are they still practicing that skill? Or is it in some way just confirming for themselves "I can do this, I am competent at this"? I make note of all this and then use it in my teaching.

TEACHING THE WAY CHILDREN LEARN

This close-up look at the morning meeting in Ronnie's class depicts children learning basic skills and content knowledge while also learning how to understand, think critically, and think deeply. At the same time, their dispositions for lifelong learning and social/emotional growth were being nurtured. The teaching practices that support this kind of multifaceted learning include

- Using rich, educative materials as resources and references for learning
- Infusing skill development into meaningful, purposeful content
- Using the diversity of learners as a resource
- Building on children's interests and offering them choices
- Creating a safe, respectful community
- Using assessment to inform teaching

These elements of teaching and learning are not, however, exclusive property of the small portion of the school day that the morning meeting occupies. As Ronnie put it:

> The whole point of the routines is that it's an everyday thing. It's something that the kids are actually living and really learning. They use what happens there to apply to other learning.

IMPLICATIONS

The routines of the morning meeting in Ronnie's class illustrate how skill work can be artfully woven into the fabric of classroom life. This close look at them demonstrates how to help children develop the skills and knowledge of today's standards in the context of meaningful experiences that support their diverse ways of learning. In our current high-stakes accountability environment—with its emphasis on early academics, standardization, and "teaching to the test"—it is especially challenging to teach children to solve problems and create new ideas in the diverse ways we know that they need to learn (Gardner, 1983; Tomlinson, 2004). I hope that the images of Ronnie's teaching provided here inspire other ideas for how skill development can be supported without focusing exclusively on test preparation and without sacrificing support for the development of the whole child.

CHAPTER 4

Teaching for Understanding Through Active Learning

In today's high-stakes accountability environment, many teachers and schools follow prescribed curricula to meet mandates and prepare for tests. Frequently, a casualty of this approach is students' understanding of what is presented. In the race to meet pacing schedules and "cover" the curriculum, children often end up with superficial understandings of the content or, worse yet, misconceptions that do not get revealed until later, when they flounder, confronted with more complex material. The shaky foundation put in place earlier proves to be inadequate for them to be able to construct deeper meaning about what they are learning. This happens frequently in the teaching of math, when, for example, children are taught to "carry the one" as they learn place value. Because the meaning of the one (a 10) is not emphasized in instruction, their later understanding of this concept is put at risk. And if children do not understand place value, they cannot be expected to really understand double-column addition or any other operation with numbers greater than 10.

The dilemma of "not understanding" is endemic in schools. It is noted in the decline of scores on reading tests, which, as children move up in the grades, emphasize comprehension (Jennings & Rentner, 2006; Nichols, Glass, & Berliner, 2005). It is also evident in the fields of mathematics and science, where international measures of achievement show that U.S. students are outperformed by students from most other industrialized nations (National Center for Education Statistics, 2004). Examinations of the causes for why U.S. students do so poorly point to the fact that in comparison with students in the United States, students in other countries study less material in much greater depth. The focus in countries that perform well on international assessments is on getting students to understand (Darling-Hammond, 2006).

How do we develop such an orientation with students in our own country, especially in schools that are under the greatest pressures from testing and mandated curricula—those serving children from low socioeconomic backgrounds, children of color, children who live in urban settings? How do we manage the tension between fostering children's in-depth understandings and addressing the requirements of districts and states for children to learn the knowledge and skills outlined in the standards for their grade? To address these questions, this chapter offers images of teaching based on the active nature of children's learning and descriptions of curricula that nurture children's understanding.

WHAT IS TEACHING FOR UNDERSTANDING?

Teaching for understanding helps children "uncover" their questions, conceptions, and misconceptions. It provides support for children to explore and answer their questions as well as generate new questions. Eleanor Duckworth talks about such teaching as an occasion for "the having of wonderful ideas." In her groundbreaking book by that title, Duckworth (2007/1987) explains that learning is a process of discovery, of having wonderful, new ideas. It doesn't matter if someone else had those ideas before. Coming up with wonderful ideas—and really understanding them—is the essence of pedagogy and one of the main purposes of education.

All learners can have wonderful ideas if the setting is right. And what makes the setting right is having a relevant and meaningful question to pursue. When a meaningful question is raised (it doesn't matter whether it is raised by children themselves or by the teacher—it just has to make sense to the children) all learners will tax themselves to the fullest to find an answer. Their interests will be piqued, they will generate more questions, and they will feel good about themselves for realizing that their ideas are significant (Duckworth, 2007/1987).

FINDING THE RIGHT QUESTION

The right question to pursue needs to be selected by teachers through a negotiation—between the ideas and knowledge people think are important for children to learn (standards) and the interests, questions, and enthusiasm of individual children and the group. Developing a curriculum of such questions involves skillful planning. To begin, a teacher needs to be knowledgeable about how children learn: how children of different ages and stages think, and what kinds of interests and themes are typical and appropriate for them at these different times. For example, teachers need to understand that it is common for young children to be intrigued by animals; fascinated by dinosaurs; and interested in learning about themselves, their immediate family, and their community. Also, older children, while able and willing to go deeper into investigations of those topics, are also curious about many other things in the bigger world, such as figuring out how things work, the rules humans make, and the nature of people and places far away and long ago.

To determine the ideas and themes best suited to children in different grades, teachers at the Bronx New School meet in cross-grade, discipline-based committees to map out the most appropriate ways for each grade level to address state standards. The teachers discuss not only the content to be introduced but also the big ideas that they want children to grapple with—some of which are called for by the standards, some of which are included by the teachers because they are valued by the school (for example, dispositions and other affective goals, such as a love of learning, compassion for others, responsibility, and hard work) and go beyond the purview of the standards. Teacher meetings also focus on how to ensure that there will be continuity of learning from one grade to another. Meetings of teachers within each grade are held regularly to discuss how each teacher will work out the details of infusing the standards of the different disciplines into a coherent and interesting curriculum.

While each class on a grade focuses on the same standards, the way the curriculum is shaped and developed throughout the year differs among teachers in each class. The curriculum varies depending on the approach of the individual teacher (influenced by his or her particular interests and strengths), the issues raised by the children in response to the big ideas presented by the teachers, and the interests children bring to bear on the topic. Thus, curriculum does not happen in isolation from the learners who are involved with it. Their questions, understandings/misunderstandings, and interests—as reflected through class discussions, projects, papers, and other activities—shape and direct its course.

CONTEXTS FOR UNDERSTANDING

To teach for understanding, it is necessary for teachers to create a context for learning that fosters exploration of the ideas and themes considered important for all to know. The context needs to be set up in a way that suggests "the having of wonderful ideas." Such an environment is rich with interesting materials and offers opportunities for what David Hawkins (1965) called "messing about" with them. It is an environment that also provides a variety of other "firsthand" learning experiences—trips, conversations with others, interviews with experts, and so on. "Children don't look closer without the reality of experience, without their own personal involvement with the experience" (Weber, 1991, p. 3).

Classrooms at the Bronx New School offer an image of what a classroom designed for teaching for understanding looks like. The rooms have tables, rather than individual desks, that can be pushed together when needed, for work on group projects. Shelves are used to define different areas and house materials for use in the study of different subjects: books in a library area; manipulatives for math; different kinds of paper, pencils, and markers for writing; paints and other supplies for art; cooking utensils and other equipment for science. Classrooms are often homes for animals, such as snakes, hamsters, rabbits, turtles, or fish. A block area is part of the classroom, too, even in the upper grades. And water and sand tables, long considered staples only of early childhood classrooms, can be found in the classrooms of the upper grades as well. Used in the younger grades for open-ended exploration, they provide opportunities for older children to engage in more directed firsthand investigation of natural phenomena, such as learning about the properties of different liquids or how islands are really underwater mountains. A rug in each room defines a meeting area, which in many classrooms includes an inviting sofa or several benches. The surrounding wall space is always covered with maps, charts that document class discussions, and other print materials developed in the course of class studies. And on the walls of every part of the room children's artwork and writing is displayed. Everything in the classroom has an educative purpose. (See Figure 4.1.)

FIGURE 4.1.

Group work at tables

Library area

FIGURE 4.1 (continued)

Math area

Art and writing center

Block area

Science table

Meeting area

TEACHING STRATEGIES FOR UNDERSTANDING

Rather than trying to cover lots of material, teaching for understanding emphasizes the notion that "less is more" (Sizer, 1984). It provides for in-depth study that involves reflecting, weighing issues and ideas, working through many options, and examining something from many different angles and through a multiplicity of lenses. Because teachers who teach for understanding know that learners often move in and out of understanding before ideas take form and crystallize, they provide their students with repeated opportunities to work deeply and for long spans of time in areas of interest, to return and to revisit these interests, to get to know each other's ideas through conversation during the course of the day, and to use each other's knowledge through peer teaching. They give children time to grapple with "wrong ideas" or "mistakes." But rather than correcting these "mistakes," teachers use them as windows into children's thinking. They use children's misconceptions to raise questions that create conflict in children's thinking. This conflict can be the source of a shift in thinking that leads children to deeper understandings.

Instead of blaming learners for not knowing, teachers who aim for understanding take responsibility for helping learners rethink their system of thoughts. They help children see where their answers hold up and where they don't, consider alternatives, and develop new solutions to a problem. In this way teachers help children push their thinking to the limit and come honestly to terms with their own ideas.

Teachers who teach for understanding realize that you can give the "right" answer, but if a person doesn't own it, that answer will often have little meaning. They understand that getting children to examine their misconceptions helps them to master what they know more deeply and is far more productive than if there never were any misconceptions to begin with.

Providing supports for this kind of learning takes time. But it is worth the time spent because it leads to a teaching that is generative, that "extends thought in new, even unanticipated ways and provides for students a deeper entry into the world" (Perrone, 1991, p. 21). This is a kind of teaching that does not try to make things simple but recognizes the value of a learner's struggle with difficult and complex ideas.

> Just as the poet seeks to present his thoughts and feelings in all their complexity, and in so doing opens a multiplicity of paths into his meaning, likewise a teacher who presents a subject matter in all its complexity makes it more accessible by opening a multiplicity of paths into it. . . . Whether it be poems, mathematical situations, historical

documents, liquids, or music, [teachers'] offerings must provide some accessible entry points, must present the subject matter from different angles, elicit different responses from different learners, open a variety of paths for exploration, engender conflicts, and provide surprises; we must encourage learners to open out beyond themselves, and help them realize that there are other points of view yet to be uncovered—that they have not yet exhausted the thoughts they might have about this matter. (Duckworth, 1991, pp. 9, 13)

WHAT TEACHERS NEED TO KNOW TO TEACH FOR UNDERSTANDING

To teach for understanding, teachers need knowledge of content, of content-pedagogy, of their students, and of how to use all these different kinds of knowledge to design a curriculum for understanding.

Knowing the Ways into Content Learning

It is commonly argued in discussions about teacher quality that teachers need to have a good grasp of the content of the disciplines that they are going to teach. However, because teachers of young children must teach all the disciplines, I would argue that they do not need to be "experts" in any one content area. Rather, they need to understand the big ideas of the subject matter at hand and know where to gain access to resources for learning about it. What they really need to know are ways into the subjects so that they can engage their learners and keep them going on to ask and answer further questions. Also of importance is for teachers to be enthusiastic learners as they engage side by side with their students. A teacher who is curious, embraces the unexpected, engages in inquiry and reflection, has intellectual passion, and exhibits a general interest in the world is a powerful model for children about what it means to be a learner.

Knowing Content-Pedagogy Well

Teachers also need what Lee Shulman (1987) calls "pedagogical-content knowledge"—effective content-specific strategies and methods for teaching different subject matter and skills. The definition of what exactly effective content pedagogy is, however, especially in the areas of literacy and mathematics, is often quite controversial. Debates rage about what approaches are most effective, but what rarely is raised in discussions of these differences is how notions of effectiveness are influenced by educators' goals, values, and views about the purposes of education (as discussed in Chapter 2). These notions of effectiveness, in turn, affect their philosophical and theoretical orientation to their teaching and research (the choice of the methods that they use, the design of studies used to determine the methods' effectiveness, and indeed the definitions of what they are actually teaching and researching). If, for example, we hold to the notion of learning as being merely the transmission of information that must be "covered" in predetermined spans of time, then what is considered to be effective content-pedagogy will most likely emphasize teaching methods that get learners to reproduce that conveyed information. However, if definitions of learning include learners' capacities to understand deeply, apply their knowledge, make connections, and examine critically, then teaching methods will emphasize skills and dispositions that support these goals.

Definitions of reading and the research on reading provide an instructive example of the complexities involved in determining what effective content-pedagogy is. For example, one definition of *reading* heavily emphasizes the ability of young readers to distinguish sounds and symbols. Those who hold this view assess children's reading abilities by testing those skills. One popular test of early reading based on such a definition makes judgments about children's reading expertise by examining how well the children sound out nonsense words (Good & Kaminski, 2002). Of course, those "trained" to recognize these meaningless sounds and syllables, when compared with those who aren't trained in such a way, do better on this type of test. So this definition of reading, which focuses on isolated symbols and word sounds, ignoring meaning, favors teaching techniques and tests of effectiveness that also focus on sounds and symbols isolated from meaning.

In contrast, when definitions of reading emphasize readers' abilities to understand what they are reading, teaching strategies and tests of effectiveness look very different. They focus on helping readers make sense of what they are reading by using a wide range of cues in the text—semantic, syntactic, and phonetic. Because this definition of reading is so much more complex, it needs to be nurtured and assessed in more complex ways to produce information about what sense readers make of what they read. What reveals this information best are observational and descriptive assessments, many of which have, in turn, contributed important understandings over the past several decades about how children actually learn to read and have subsequently shaped even further definitions of effective content-pedagogy (as well as suitable assessments and research studies).

In other words, research of practice has led to new knowledge for practice; this new knowledge then gets fed back into teaching, producing yet more knowledge about what constitutes literacy, literacy learning, and good teaching. The process is an iterative cycle that is affected by perspectives and definitions. When the definition of reading includes comprehension, teaching strategies and assessments emphasize comprehension; when the definition of reading is limited to recognition of sounds and symbols isolated from the context of their meaning, that is what gets taught and tested.

The larger point that I am trying to make here is that one's definition of effective content pedagogy is shaped by one's views about learning and what constitutes valid assessment of that learning. Good content-pedagogy, like most things in life, is influenced by one's values, purposes, and philosophical orientations. My view of learning, guided by knowledge of how children learn (that they construct knowledge through active involvement with the world), as well as my view of the purpose of education (to understand and make meaning of the world), shapes what I see as effective content-pedagogy and curriculum development. I believe that good teachers are clear about these issues. They choose teaching and assessment strategies to match their vision and their purposes.

Knowing Students Well

Teachers who value their students' understanding also value knowing their students well. They learn about their students by being careful listeners and observers. Through listening and observing they learn about how and what children understand, what areas of learning are in need of support, what children's interests are, what the purposes for their work are, and what their unique learning styles and strengths are. Teachers who keep track of these things and note them regularly are able to raise questions that make sense to children, to think of orientations for activities that correspond to their way of seeing things, and to gain a picture of each child and his or her growth that can be used over time to guide further teaching.

USING KNOWLEDGE OF STUDENTS, CONTENT, AND CONTENT PEDAGOGY TO DESIGN A CURRICULUM FOR UNDERSTANDING

Susan, a 4th-grade teacher from the Bronx New School's earlier years, does this kind of careful observation and documentation of what children do, how they approach their work, and what strategies they use when doing it. She keeps ongoing records of individual students as well as a record of the discussions of the whole class. She collects samples of children's work in portfolios. Documenting children's learning in this way helps her to see the children's strengths—what they *can* do—rather than focus on their deficits—what they *can't* do. This enables her to see how her students develop and integrate their understandings.

Susan uses the knowledge of her students gained through her observations to shape and guide her curriculum. Her planning process goes something like this: She starts with a general review of the city/state standards to map out the big areas of study that she wants to pursue over the course of the school year. She chooses which area of study to introduce first and then she prepares her environment to support the themes and ideas she plans to bring into the classroom. She familiarizes herself with the literature related to the ideas and themes and then makes decisions about where to begin: what story to read first; what books and materials to put out; what idea to introduce first. She sets up a schedule for the day that provides a mix of individual work time, small-group time, and whole-group meetings. She also organizes the room to maximize children's abilities to be independent in their learning: What areas will be where? Where will all the materials go? Where will children store their notebooks, folders, and supplies?

Susan also sets up a system for her own record keeping: how she will document each child's reading, writing, math, and other interdisciplinary projects. She develops a schedule for conferencing individually with each child about reading, writing, and math and for meeting with small "guided reading" groups that she configures for various purposes (Pinnell & Fountas, 1996). And she sets aside time to reflect on the growth of individual children as well as on what she learns about the group during whole-class discussions. She uses all this information to make decisions about how to shape each subsequent step of the curriculum. Her planning is thus an interplay between required expectations and what she learns from the children about their understandings in the course of the curriculum. What follows are some images of some studies that have taken place in Susan's 4th-grade classroom.

The Flight Curriculum: Developing Understanding Through Active Learning

The Flight Curriculum in Susan's class was designed to address state standards in science, social studies, and English Language Arts. It was initiated by a trip to the Intrepid, a navy aircraft carrier docked at a pier on New York City's Hudson River that is now a museum. After the trip, many students began building planes out of junk materials during the class "work time," a period offered several times a week that allowed children, individually and in groups, to actively engage with materials and projects. The children based their constructions on information learned during their trip as well as on research from books about aviation and flight that Susan had brought into the classroom. Among the vehicles they built were the Universal, the stealth bomber, the Intruder, a glider, and helicopters. These creations were shared at all-class meetings held immediately after work time—a time when children presented what they had learned during their work time investigations. The sharing was usually followed by children's observations, comments, questions, or suggestions about one another's work.

For example, when Hassan shared what he had read about how the design of planes had changed over time, someone asked him, "Why did some of the early two-seater planes have the pilot sit in a backseat?" This question, which he was unable to answer, inspired him to revisit his reading during a subsequent work time to fill in the details that he did not know. Or when Anthony shared what he was learning about aerodynamics from the paper air vehicles that he was making, someone in the class asked him, "How does a helicopter go forward?" This question motivated him to experiment more with making paper helicopters until he actually understood how they worked.

In response to children's questions and interests, Susan brought in books about paper airplanes, which inspired even more students in the class to get involved in making them. As they constructed different kinds of planes they struggled with such questions as "What's the best paper?" "What's the best design?" "How does a helicopter go forward?"

Susan extended the work for some of the children by asking them to make blueprints and maps of their constructions. Presentations of these projects at class meetings led to even more questions: "How is a helicopter made?" "How is a medical helicopter different from a regular helicopter?" These questions, in turn, led to discussions of a more philosophical nature: "What does 'regular' mean?"

Susan helped the children to construct their understandings by reflecting their knowledge back to them. She wrote down their questions, observations, and comments on big charts that she hung on the walls of the meeting area for all the children to see. "I would scribe these ideas because otherwise they would get lost," said Susan. Sometimes she would even type these notes and distribute them at the next day's meeting. In this way Susan served as keeper of the children's memories (kind of like what a good parent does). She reflected questions and answers back to the children and picked up the pieces of their learning, reminding them about what they already knew and helping them to connect their ideas to the big ideas of the world. She did this because she understood that children often do not realize all that they actually know until it is pointed out to them. She also knew that seeing their work in the context of others' would help them make sense of what they were doing.

The understandings gained during the Flight Curriculum were recorded on a chart that stayed posted on the walls of the classroom throughout the study. Titled "Our Learning About Airplanes, Helicopters and How They Fly," it read:

- The way the blades on a fan are positioned affects how the air flows.
- Air makes things float.
- Propellers on top of helicopters are called rotors. They turn and pull the helicopter up. It goes up like a tornado.
- The helicopter flies at an angle to make it go forward. The forces from the front and back equalize it.
- The rudder and tail can change a plane's direction. The rudder catches the wind and pulls the plane back.
- Whether a plane flies or crashes depends on the design and the material it's made of. It's kind of like floating and sinking.
- 1919—the 1st Trans-Atlantic flight by Alcock & Brown.
- The Cessna plane is a sports plane.
- The Intruder plane was a bomber plane used in Vietnam.
- We should recycle planes.
- The early planes were made of canvas, bamboo and wood. They were bi-planes and tri-planes. They had no propellers.
- The stealth bomber moves by thrust.
- The Universal plane was the first to use radar. It was made in WWII.
- A future transporter plane will be solar powered with an electric battery storage system.

The class reviewed this chart regularly throughout the course of the curriculum. Each time they reviewed it they discussed what they were learning, what additional information they needed in order to continue their studies, and what they needed to do to move forward in pursuit of their questions. As they used the chart they learned to distinguish what was true from what was false and they learned to differentiate between opinions and facts. Susan reflects on these discussions:

These discussions were the most exciting part of our day. I never knew where a conversation was going to take us. I never knew where a day would end and what we were all going to get out of it. The work seemed to literally generate itself. (Falk & Blumenreich, 2005, p. 169)

The Bubble Study: Moving From the Concrete to the Abstract

Whenever possible, Susan tried to help children learn through investigations that involve "hands-on" explorations. She encouraged them to learn as much as possible from firsthand observations and experimentations (just as serious scientists do) rather than relying solely on books or other outside information. She did this because she understood that books—which have the potential to raise questions, get children intrigued with something, point to particular phenomenon, and provide lots of facts—can also get in the way of children's understanding if children consult them before they have had the concrete experiences needed to ensure that the explanations make sense.

Susan's class's Bubble Study is an example of how to use concrete experiences to move children toward more abstract understandings. It began with opportunities provided during work time for children to explore bubbles at the water table, observe and document what they were doing, and raise questions about the properties of bubbles—their strength, size, structure, and colors. At the conclusion of each work time the class met to share developing observations and raise new questions. The questions, which were recorded on large chart paper that hung on the walls in the meeting area, helped to shape plans for the next few days' work.

By following the progression of the children's ideas, Susan gradually introduced other materials and ideas. For example, the class examined solutions; layers in solutions; the chemistry of baking; "mystery" powders; and what happens when salt, heat, or both are added to different materials. However, it was bubbles that seemed to most powerfully capture the children's interests. They returned to their investigations time after time, excitedly discussing findings, answering questions, and generating new questions they hadn't thought of before. When they explored everything they could think of, and everything that Susan could think of, they decided to write a class book about what they had learned. Titling it *The Bubble Book*, they put it together by first going through the charts that had recorded their observations and questions throughout the study. Next, they discussed what they had discovered, deciding together about what information was true and what was false. Only after they finished this process did they consult all the books about bubbles that they could find. To their surprise and delight, they found out that through their own experimentation, they had already discovered most of the facts about bubbles that were in the published books. They wrote down what they wanted to convey and published the book on the computer, complete with illustrations. This class-produced book helped the children, amazed by this documentation of all they knew, rid themselves of some of the remnants of traditional notions of learning, which many still carried from their earlier school experiences, that learning is solely about receiving information from teachers and books. They dubbed the process they had gone through "reverse learning" (see Figure 4.2).

Susan had a great time with these class studies. Throughout, she was a learner right alongside her students, bringing her own curiosity to their investigations, never hesitating to put out her own ideas for them to come up against or to argue with—"Gee, I wonder if . . . " or "I don't understand; can you explain what you mean?"—but always careful not to simply supply them with the "right" answers. She asked questions to elucidate the nature of their thinking. Consciously avoiding questions about "why" (so complex and hard to answer), she asked open-ended questions that gave them something else to try, something to get them going again: "Have you seen anything new? What do you think happens if? What can you do to make that happen again? What did you do that was different from last time? Could you make a drawing to show what you did?" Can you find a way . . . ? (Harlen, 2001; Osborne & Freyberg, 1985).

Remaining cautious about not letting her ideas dominate, she tried to extend and bring enthusiasm to the children's investigations. She herself often did not know the answer to the question the children were pursuing. Rather than seeking the answer herself and then giving it to them, she identified materials and resources that could be used by the children to investigate the question on their own and take their study to a deeper level. Reflecting on this phenomenon, she told me:

> I was a learner just like the kids. I didn't have all the answers. In fact, when a study of a particular topic took hold in the room, the way I found out about it was to read as much as I could find in all the "kid books," the Internet, and the encyclopedia. If the kids needed to go deeper in pursuit of their questions, they called an expert or we went to a museum.

What did the children think about learning in this way? Their reflections, which I jotted down during a visit to a class discussion, reveal their thoughts and their feelings:

> Instead of reading about something, you do it and because you want to learn about something, you try hard and learn more.

FIGURE 4.2. The Bubble Book

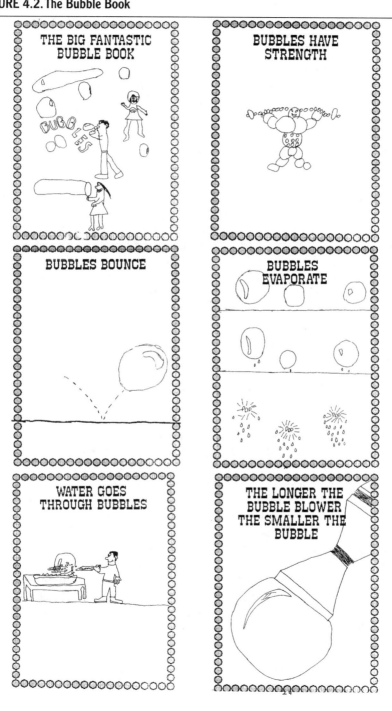

When you are interested in something you don't learn about that subject because someone tells you the answers; you study it and learn it in your own way.

In most schools you get told what to do and what to know but never get your questions answered. In this class you get help to find answers to your questions so you feel better about asking them.

Through this way of working in Susan's class, each child was able to find an area in which he or she excelled; children also became valued by the others as an "expert" in their area of strength. This valuing of their strengths helped the children learn to appreciate each other. For example, when the children were publishing *The Bubble Book*, Santiago—known as the prolific writer of the group—worked closely with Akeem—who struggled with reading and writing but had remarkable drawing skills. Their collaboration broke the hold of the inner and outer circle of academic success that is prevalent in so many classroom settings (the distinction between "smart" and "not-so-smart" kids). The children explained it in this way:

We learn not only from ourselves, but from other people's ideas and find information from each other.

This class brings out your talents.

CHALLENGES FOR TEACHERS
WHO TEACH FOR UNDERSTANDING

Developing a curriculum for understanding presents teachers with many challenges. It requires a shift in the teacher's traditional role from being a giver of information and a provider of answers to being an observer of children and a facilitator of their learning. Instead of the teacher's job being to explain things to students, it is, rather, to try to understand the sense children are making about what they are learning and help them find their way to their own understanding. This shift thus calls on teachers to listen to children's voices closely, to value what they know as well as what they don't know, and to take responsibility for finding a way to get them all to a place where they genuinely understand.

It is hard to teach for understanding, especially in today's high-stakes testing environment. It takes time for learners to really develop understandings, about simple as well as complex ideas. And in addition, the overwhelming amount of things teachers are expected to do each day with their classes, the prescribed curricula, and the pacing schedules that dictate the page the class must be on each day, make it difficult for teachers to do the kind of in-depth work that is necessary to support children's thinking. However, in the final analysis, it is not how fast children progress through a curriculum that counts, but how far they go toward understanding that curriculum. If we want children to truly own what they learn, there really is no other choice for teachers than to focus on enhancing children's understandings.

CHAPTER 5

Integrating the Curriculum:
Making Connections Between Ideas

Children learn through active engagement with materials, each other, and adults. They learn when they are involved in experiences that have meaning to them. They learn about the world in an integrated way. To them, reading, math, science, and social studies are not separate topics but, instead, indistinguishable pieces of everyday life.

This chapter offers an image of teaching at the Bronx New School that helps children make connections between ideas by integrating learning across the disciplines. As children engaged in the mix of experiences described, they were exposed to important knowledge and skills across the different disciplines. However, because the learning did not label the different disciplines in neatly packaged, subtitled headings to which we adults are so accustomed, many families at the school did not, at first, recognize the learning that was actually taking place. Their confusion was exacerbated by the fact that the activities felt so enjoyable to the children and involved so many real-life experiences. But this was the goal in the Bronx New School's early days—to create a place that lessened the boundaries between the learning that goes on in everyday life and the learning that goes on in school.

As time went by, learning through the integration of the disciplines—with activities that were meaningful and purposeful, interesting and enjoyable—became more recognizable and acceptable to all. To help explain and build support for this kind of work, I documented the full progression of the interdisciplinary, extended study that follows. It took place in one classroom during one school year. This is my description of the Undersea Study, which was experienced by the children in Sue's class.

THE UNDERSEA STUDY: AN INTEGRATED INVESTIGATION

Sue's 2nd-grade class conducted numerous extended studies over the course of one school year—of human families and homes, of animal homes, of folk tales, of how bridges work, of how plants grow from seeds. Artifacts from these could be seen all over her classroom, which was furnished with tables and chairs arranged in centers separated by clearly labeled shelves packed with teacher- and student-made materials for literacy, art, math, and science. Jars of water brewing experiments, trays of germinating seeds and plants, batteries and bulbs, a scale, as well as aquarium tanks (one with a turtle, the other with fish) occupied the shelf surfaces and windowsills. A rug, delineating a meeting area, was placed in the classroom library area, which contained a book display case and several bookshelves housing a wide range of children's fiction, content area books, and reference materials—some organized by difficulty level, some by categories of interest. Classroom walls were covered with children's drawings, writings from their various studies, as well as charts, graphs, maps, and posters (see Figure 5.1).

FIGURE 5.1.

Math center

Meeting area

Computer area

Initially Sue had planned to address the standards for her grade through a theme of homes—for people and animals. Early in the year, when a parent gifted the class with a water turtle, this fit right in and the class set up a habitat for the turtle. They visited a pet store, where they bought an aquarium and other related equipment. They also bought goldfish, which, they learned at the store, were what the turtle liked to eat. When they fed these to the turtle, it gobbled them alive, much to everyone's horror and delight. This event triggered a flurry of writings and drawings re-creating the gory scene. It also ignited a curiosity about fish and other undersea phenomena.

Such was the origin of the Undersea Study. It grew out of the children's intense interest in fish, especially the interests of one little boy, Kobe. Before the arrival of the turtle, he had experienced difficultly engaging in sustained activities and getting along with other children. However, his interest in watching, drawing, and looking at books about fish dramatically transformed his behavior. Before this study he had been unable to sit still, even for a short period of time. But when the fish arrived in the classroom, he began to spend hours observing and documenting them as well as perusing the many books about them that Sue had made sure to bring into the classroom. Using markers, pen and ink, Craypas, and paints, he produced colorful, detailed portraits of them. At about the same time, he also started participating in class meetings, demonstrating to the other children the wealth of knowledge he had about fish.

Curious about how Kobe knew so much about this topic, Sue mentioned it to his mother at their home–school conference. It was at this meeting that Kobe's mom revealed they had a tropical aquarium at home. She offered to help Sue set one up in the classroom. Initially hesitant to start this project, worrying that she did not know enough to do it properly and a bit wary of working with Kobe's mother, with whom she had previously had a rocky relationship because of disagreements over how to discipline Kobe for his challenging behavior, Sue relented and agreed to give it a try. She and Kobe's mom thus began a partnership that not only aided the development of the class curriculum but also sent a message to Kobe about cooperation and trust between home and school. I am convinced that this message is, in part, what helped him manage his behavior better and become integrated more fully into the classroom community.

In the course of the aquarium project, the class made numerous trips back to the neighborhood pet shop to purchase tropical fish and more equipment. They read books about fish and spent hours observing and documenting what the fish did. They visited the aquatic dioramas at the American Museum of Natural History, after which they created their own aquatic dioramas. They also made a trip to an exhibit of Alexander Calder's fish mobiles at the Whitney Museum of Art. On their return they made their own mobiles of fish figures stuffed with paper.

In spite of the richness of these experiences, Sue felt she could extend the study more. So she took the class on a trip to the Northwind Undersea Institute, a marine museum in a neighboring Bronx community. The information the class was exposed to there led to a study of ocean life, pollution, and other issues related to the environment. Following the trip, Sue brought books about the ocean into the classroom. She also introduced experiments to help the children understand different aspects of the ocean: about the different temperature zones in the different sea levels, the increasing strength of water as the ocean levels deepen, how to measure water pressure, and how sound waves travel in water. The interest and excitement generated by these experiments spread to all the children in the classroom, even Caleb, another child who in the past had been really disruptive and difficult to get along with.

As the children worked on these experiments, they continued to observe and record the action in the aquarium tanks, perused countless books and magazines about underwater life, and had many discussions about the information they were accumulating and the understandings they were developing. At the suggestion of Sophia, still another child in the class with challenging behavior, the children wrote a play called "Life Under the Sea." Each class member wrote a story and made a puppet about an ocean creature or element. Then they put all the stories together, designed the scenery, and acted out the parts. From this play Sue discovered how much the children, especially the quieter ones in the class, had absorbed from their study.

Working with the Undersea Study's variety of engaging media and activities helped all the children learn a lot, especially those who had difficulties. Sophia, the girl who originally suggested the play, was someone who got really involved. She assumed leadership and provided direction to others, departing from her previous stance as a "troublemaker," a role Sue long suspected Sophia had adopted to mask the fact that she struggled as a reader and writer. As a result of her intense work on the script, not only did Sophia's behavior improve, but her literacy development also took a leap forward.

None of this happened by accident, though. Throughout the study Sue paid close attention to the "grade level" skills and content children needed to know. She took every opportunity that she could to infuse the teaching of needed skills and facts into the context of the curriculum. During literacy time, for example, she introduced readings related to the ocean, fish, turtles, habitats, and the environment. She had the children work on their writing by doing written responses to the readings, making charts at class meetings, and creating stories about the topic they studied. She wove skill work related to other content areas into the various activities, creating mini-lessons as the need arose for individuals as well as groups. (When it was not possible to teach all required content like this, other activities—both individual and group—were designed to make sure that standards were being addressed.)

At the culmination of the study the children presented an "Ocean Museum" to their families and the other children in the school. This "museum" took the form of an exhibition held in the classroom. Here the children showcased their projects; demonstrated the experiments they had completed; and displayed the writings, drawings, and dioramas they had made. There were four different "hands-on" water experiments as well as activities for the visitors to try, such as making their own version of a stuffed fish mobile—all developed by the children during their study.

During this Ocean Museum the children also presented their puppet show to their visitors. Photos were taken of the event, which, at the study's end, the class used to create a book documenting the progression of their learning during the study. It was compiled by asking each child to choose a photo from among those taken during the study and to write a caption for it. When these were completed, the class got together to reminisce about, analyze, and reflect on their work. They commented on each other's writings, offering additional information and making suggestions for the book's final version. This record of their curriculum's development was placed in the library beside other books made by the children to document their classroom studies. There it stayed for the children to review as a testament to their collective inquiry.

THE POWER OF TEACHING TO CHILDREN'S INTERESTS

The Undersea Study was born out of the children's interests and shaped by their questions. Sue took these seriously and used them to continually shape the curriculum. The more she did this, the more the children got involved and participated in the work. In one discussion I had with Sue, she talked about the impact of her actions:

> I used to plan out all the activities of a thematic study in advance. The kids were assigned projects to do. They would finish them and then come to me and say, "All right, what do I have to do next?" But when I began to follow the lead of their interests, I

stopped getting that question from them. The kids had an enthusiasm and motivation that kept them going on their own. It was then that I realized children have their own work, and that what a teacher has to do is recognize this and provide children with the opportunity to do it.

Others have discussed this notion that Sue realized. Patricia Carini, the founder of the Prospect School in Vermont, known for its documentary processes about children and their work, wrote:

> It is, I would hold, deep and compelling interest in something, a valuing of it, that releases productivity and opens a path for continued work and contribution. . . . What the child strongly prefers, what the child freely chooses, are the things and ideas for which he or she has feeling and affection. What we feel deeply about, what we have a feeling for, draws us to it. We wonder about it. We question it. We explore it. We become immersed in it. It evokes our thought. This, I believe, is the impetus to learning and knowledge: to be drawn to and to be drawn forth. (1987, p. 7)

Few individuals reject work connected to their interest or related to a purpose that they consider important. In fact, when learners are given the opportunity to pursue their own interests, not only are they able to learn in depth, but their motivation to learn is enhanced along the way. The drive to learn, what some say is a drive all humans are born with (Shonkoff & Phillips, 2000), is actually fueled by interest. When interest is present in the learning environment, there is less need for external rewards and punishments—not only to motivate learning but to motivate behavior as well. Only when learning is presented as external to the interests and motivation of the learner does it need to rely on privileges, rewards, and punishment to maintain focus and obedience (Kamii, 1985). In such cases—still sadly the norm in most schools—children are told what and when to learn and the school day is filled with rules they must obey. In contrast, when children's interests are infused into the curriculum, their independence and autonomy flourish. They are more intrinsically motivated, not only to learn, but to behave cooperatively as well. Discipline problems seem to fade away.

BUILDING ON CHILDREN'S STRENGTHS

The more children are allowed to pursue their interests, the more visible their strengths become. They are then able to use these strengths to get more involved in their work.

To teach from strength is to teach in the light of the child's preferred learning mode according to the shape of his or her thought, and with attention to what is of deep interest and value to the child. This is observable wherever the learning environment provides the child with the opportunity to engage with a range of media and materials to which the child can give shape and form; and the opportunity to contribute ideas and raise questions that will be heard and responded to. (Carini, 1986, p. 20)

Sue's teaching, as exemplified in the Undersea Study, encouraged the children to explore their thinking and to solve problems, by engaging not only with a wide range of materials, but also in a wide range of ways—through reading and writing as well as through talking, building, or doing art. Working in these different modalities allowed the children to express their own unique talents and ways of seeing and being in the world. In response, Sue took note of their different learning styles and strengths, finding ways to use these in the curriculum. This gave the children confidence, especially those who were insecure about their abilities. Some tried things they had not previously been successful at or were reluctant to do in other contexts.

MAKING ROOM FOR ALL KINDS OF LEARNERS

Howard Gardner (1983) uses the term "multiple intelligences" to describe the many different sorts of potentials that people possess. He argues that intelligence, as it is traditionally defined and identified through IQ tests, does not adequately encompass the wide variety of abilities that human beings possess. In his conception, there is not one but nine intelligences: linguistic, logical-mathematical, spatial, bodily-kinesthetic, musical, interpersonal, intrapersonal, naturalistic, and existential (Gardner, 2006).

Following Gardner's theory, it becomes apparent that schools generally value only the linguistic and logical-mathematical intelligences and make judgments that children who are strong in these areas are more intelligent than other children. For example, a child who becomes a fluent reader early or masters the multiplication tables easily is often considered to be more intelligent than a child who struggles in these areas. What is not considered, however, is that the second child may be stronger in another *kind* of intelligence, and therefore may best learn the given material through a different approach; or that the child may excel in a different field; or that the child may even be looking at reading or mathematics in a different way that hides a potentially higher intelligence than the one who masters these skills more easily. Gardner's theory suggests then that, rather than relying on a uniform curriculum weighted toward linguistic and logical-mathematical abilities, schools need to differentiate the curricula to be responsive to the individual proclivities of each child, teaching in ways that will nurture the diverse talents of all children.

Maxine Greene echoes this need to respect many kinds of learning modalities:

> Each [learner] is a perspective after all; each provides a new opportunity for structuring experience; each offers a distinctive lens through which to attend to the lived, intersubjective world. (1984, p. 16)

In many schools, learning differences are associated with deficits and are attended to through separation mechanisms—tracking, gifted programs, special education, grade retention, and restrictive admission policies based on skill-related definitions of school readiness. While the use of these practices is often rationalized by claims that they equitably attend to individual differences, in reality these practices often highlight students' deficits rather than support their strengths. The result is that an increasing number of children are considered out of the bounds of what is considered normal. More and more are referred to special services or held over in a grade. Children who are successful in conventional ways do all right. But those who diverge from the increasingly narrow definitions of normalcy often are provided with few opportunities to learn in ways that are suited to their needs. Not only does their performance suffer, but so does their self-esteem.

The children in Sue's class were supported and respected for their individual strengths and their diverse ways of learning. Because Sue knew each one of them well, she allowed them to work at their own pace and difficulty level. No one "right" way to do things was held up; rather, there was an open-ended, flexible appreciation for multiple ways of approaching and thinking about issues as well as multiple ways of showing what they knew. In class meetings, Sue welcomed different strategies and solutions to problems. She recognized that one person's strategy might open up an understanding for another and that the children's process of explaining their ideas to others helped them to articulate and solidify their thinking. The more she did this the more children learned to ask each other questions and rely on each other to work things through. As they shared information and helped each other find resources and learn new skills, a sense of community developed in the class. Their questions often led to bigger questions that carried across different units of study.

CURRICULUM INTEGRATION

Alfred North Whitehead, the educational philosopher, once said, "In separation all meaning evaporates" (1959, p. 133). The learning that took place in Sue's classroom was not artificially separated into distinct fields or subject matters. It was connected to real life, intertwined and interconnected, containing possibilities for multiple interpretations and multiple entry points. Sue helped her students use the thinking that evolved out of this work to connect up to other big, important ideas. In this way, the children expanded their thinking and deepened their understandings.

Working in such a way suggests a new notion of the term "integrated curriculum." It is a notion that reconceptualizes curriculum as an opportunity for awakening and pursuing questions, an opportunity for each learner to discover and integrate knowledge in his or her own way. In this conception, integration of learning is an act of the learner, not a presentation of the teacher. This is very different from what happens with traditional curricula where everyone is given the same information to process in the exact same way; where the sense-making and connections have already been done by the writers of the curriculum before being given to the students to "learn."

The integrated curriculum for understanding described in this chapter challenges children to construct and synthesize their own understandings. It is *they* who integrate the curriculum as they actively engage with materials and ideas, discover the relatedness of events, and make connections between their experiences.

CHAPTER 6

Nurturing Children to Become Critical Thinkers

An integrated curriculum is a powerful vehicle to help children learn about critical thinking. This chapter examines the unfolding of an integrated curriculum, focusing on the strategies that the teacher used to nurture children's abilities to analyze, synthesize, and think critically. It describes a 14-week study of Colonial New York that Martha did with her fifth-grade class at the Bronx New School. Martha and I (along with colleagues Tom Hatch and Kristin Eno from the National Center for Restructuring Education, Schools, and Teaching at Teachers College, Columbia University) documented this curriculum project to produce a record of practice that is part of the Carnegie Foundation's *Inside Teaching* collection, a web-based archive of teaching practice that spans the disciplines in grades PreK–12 (National Center for Restructuring Education, Schools, and Teaching, 2006). I share the documentation of Martha's practice here to offer an image of how an integrated curriculum for understanding nurtures children's critical abilities to appreciate and engage with different perspectives, understand that there are a variety of ways to influence the opinions of others, and develop a sense of autonomy about their ideas.

This study was part of a yearlong plan that Martha developed with other teachers on her grade level to address their state's social studies standards. To begin, to help establish a sense of history (which is still difficult for children of that age group to understand—it often does not consolidate until children are well into their teenage years [Hallam, 1970; Zaccaria, 1978]), Martha asked the children to draw a picture of something that happened long ago. Reflecting the range of their understandings, some drew pictures of the Stone Age and some made pictures of the events of September 11, 2001. This heightened Martha's awareness of the differences in their abilities to understand what constitutes "the past." At a subsequent class meeting, she reviewed the responses together with the children, making a time line of the events they drew.

As she discussed the exercise with them, she used it to further develop their conception of long ago by emphasizing the need to be specific when discussing history, rather than simply referring to everything that has passed in the way that they typically did—as "back in the day."

ESTABLISHING A SENSE OF TIME AND PLACE

After this introduction, the study of Colonial New York took off with an exploration of the history of New Amsterdam. The initial goal was to establish an understanding of time and place. The class read a lot and took several trips to Lower Manhattan, the site of New York's early history. They visited one of the early Colonial homesteads—the Van Cortlandt Manor in the Bronx, and made a field trip to the Museum of the City of New York to see rooms depicting life during this period. Then they wrote a book together—each child writing a different section—that detailed their emerging understandings about what life in New Amsterdam was like long ago.

When that was finished, the class began a discussion of how New York changed when the British took over rule from the Dutch. The children looked at maps of the city at different points in time, went back to Lower Manhattan to visit buildings from Colonial times, and walked around the perimeter of what had been New Amsterdam. They read the British slave code as well as narrative descriptions of how lives of Africans changed under British rule.

LEARNING ABOUT THE DAILINESS OF LIFE LONG AGO

With this grounding in the context of their study, the class moved on to activities designed to help them understand daily life in Colonial America. Martha wanted to help the children learn about the jobs people had and how they got what they needed. So she put together a packet of readings that included information and resources about the different kinds of work the colonists did. After the children read the packet, she invited each child to choose a job from that time period and to research everything they could find out about it. Martha gave them a set of guiding questions to help them process the information.

Understanding that children learn best when what they study is meaningful and purposeful, Martha invited each child to create a persona for the Colonial character whose job—shoemaker, blacksmith, silversmith, merchant, and so on—they had chosen. In the course of creating their persona, the children decided that they wanted to give their person a name. To help them get a sense of what were typical names of the time period, Martha got a hold of actual census records from New York City in 1703 and brought them in for the class to see. Although her plan had been simply to review the records and then have each student select a name, the children's responses led the discussion in a different way. In relating this turn of events, Martha explained:

> I began the discussion by asking the class what they noticed about the forms. They immediately noticed the way the records were set up and what information the records showed, and then, to my surprise, instead of trying to pronounce the unusual names, or claim the names for themselves, they started to discuss what information was *not* shown. For example, there are few women's names that are given; many households had more than two adults; and there are racial designations for some of the people on the chart, but not for others. These observations led to questions, which led to several days of rich conversation and insights about what these documents tell us about the social structure of colonial New York.
>
> This experience reminded me why authentic documents are so important to share with children. It also made me think about the importance of being flexible about the directions that students want to take the class. (National Center for Restructuring Education, Schools, and Teaching, 2006, n.p.)

And Martha indeed was flexible with her plans. She did not insist on following the project plan that she had originally created. Instead, she used this initial plan as a draft that she continually revised in response to her students' developing questions.

As the class pursued their questions they also proceeded to give their characters a name and develop a personality for them. Based on what they were learning about the Colonial time period, they each described their character's family and what a day in their character's life looked like (when the character got up, what he or she did during the day, with whom the character interacted, and what kinds of tools he or she used for their work). In addition, from what they learned about the architecture of the time, the children described what the home of their person might have looked like, on the outside as well as the inside. They also invented other facts about the characters' lives: what they did for fun, why their family left England, and what interesting experiences they had had. With information gleaned from books about Colonial life forming the basis of these descriptions, the children also used their imaginations to develop their character and their character's background.

When they completed this assignment the children all interviewed each other about their jobs to get a broader sense, from the whole class, of the different people who made up the New Amsterdam community.

During the interviews, everyone walked around the room in the character of their person, introducing themselves to each other and telling each other about their lives (see Figure 6.1). Because so many interactions took place, the children got deeply into their characters, elaborating on the details of their jobs and the other information they had developed about who they were. This seemed to be a turning point in the project: The children were clearly invested in what they were doing. After about 45 minutes or so of the children walking around and talking to each other, the whole class came together for a discussion of how all the different jobs interacted with and depended on each other. They made a chart of their interdependent relationships. Here are a few examples of what they wrote:

> Student 1: I depend on the blacksmith because I need tools. I am a colonial cabinetmaker and I need tools and nails.

> Student 2: I depend on the blacksmith too because I am a farmer. I need horseshoes for my horse and wagon.

Recognizing everyone's interdependence helped the children understand the complexities of community in Colonial times. The discussion also brought other issues to their attention—what life was like for women and the African slaves of that time. These questions added another layer of complexity to their developing understandings and helped Martha address one of the important goals of the project, which was how people who held different status and power held different views and were affected differently by the same events.

FIGURE 6.1. Interviews

STUDYING HISTORICAL EVENTS: THE STANDARDS DILEMMA

Prior to this study's inception, Martha had framed the content knowledge of the state standards into questions she wanted the children to explore: Who controlled the colonists? How is this different from America today? What was mercantilism and what were its laws? Whom did mercantilism affect? How did the French-Indian War change relationships with England? How did the war affect Native Americans? Who was affected by the Navigation Acts and the Sugar Act and how? Why did the Native Americans side with the French?

In the course of the planning, however, Martha and her grade-level colleagues found managing the state standards to be a big challenge. With a scope a mile wide but only an inch deep, the teachers found the standards difficult to cover, especially because their goal was to help the children truly understand what they were studying. Martha and her team struggled with this dilemma, eventually choosing an approach that abandoned hope of covering everything in favor of doing an in-depth study that raised important content and key ideas in ways that would make sense to the children. To their surprise, however, at the conclusion of the study, when the teachers reviewed their plans in relation to the standards and to what they actually had done, they found that their in-depth work had actually ended up addressing the bulk of the ideas and information outlined in the standards. Here are some of Martha's thoughts on this:

> This city and state social studies curriculum . . . covers this humongous range of material, and to think that you could do justice to any of it in an entire year is sort of absurd. But then, doing an in-depth study like this and looking back and saying here was a point where we were comparing the governments of two countries, and finding geography in here when we were looking at the trade routes, we found the ways most of these other things were addressed in the study. (National Center for Restructuring Education, Schools, and Teaching, 2006, n.p.)

Faced with so many required subjects and standards, readers of this account must be wondering how Martha found the time to do all of what has been described here. The answer is really quite simple. She decided on what was important and then made sure to make the time to do it. Sometimes devoting so much time to social studies meant that other subjects were, as Martha explained, "put on the back burner" for a bit. But at other times she brought those other subjects forward and focused on them more intensely. It was a dance of negotiation that she orchestrated, guided by the rhythm and flow of the children's developing understandings.

DRAMATIC PLAY AS A WAY TO UNDERSTAND HISTORY

Throughout the study of Colonial New York Martha relied heavily on engaging her students in dramatic play to help them understand the important historical information of the time period. In addition to inviting children to develop the details of the lives of their assumed Colonial characters, she created a series of town meetings for their characters to attend at which they were presented with an action the British took and then asked to react to it from their characters' points of view. The first town meeting held by the class was to discuss slavery, the slave code, and indentured servants. Students played different roles as members of different social classes and discussed the fairness of these policies (see Figure 6.2).

The next few class meetings discussed taxation of the colonists by the British Government (the Townsend Act). After learning about taxes—what they were, what they were used for, how they were decided upon—the children talked about the different ways that the taxes affected the lives of the colonists and their communities. Each was asked to consider the impact of taxation on his or her Colonial character. As a result of the conversations that ensued, Martha was pleased to see that some of the children were able to get to a point where they were not just thinking about the taxes and the fact that taxation would cause them to pay more money for their purchases, but also thinking about how the decision to tax was imposed on them—that the colonists had no voice in the matter.

FIGURE 6.2. Town meeting

The conversations also revealed, however, that not everyone in the class had made it to that point. Others in the class did not fully understand the tax laws and their impact or the critical point about how a colonial government imposes its rule. Martha realized that she could not go further with the study until she helped more children to understand these issues. So she again took a detour from her plans, asking everyone to create a budget for things they needed to buy and then calculate the total price they would have to pay when the additional cost of the taxes was added. While the children worked on this problem at their tables, Martha walked around, checking in with each child and offering assistance to those who were in need of it. When the children finished their calculations and she brought them together again to discuss the comparisons they had made between the two prices, she was pleased to find that this additional exercise had made things a lot clearer for everyone.

Going back into their characters, the class was then asked, at another town meeting, to decide what they as a group would do about the taxes; what the reactions to their actions might be from the British; and, considering the consequences, whether or not each individual would actually participate in the group's decision. Martha made a chart during this discussion to document the children's thinking (see Figure 6.3).

FIGURE 6.3. Colonial New York chart

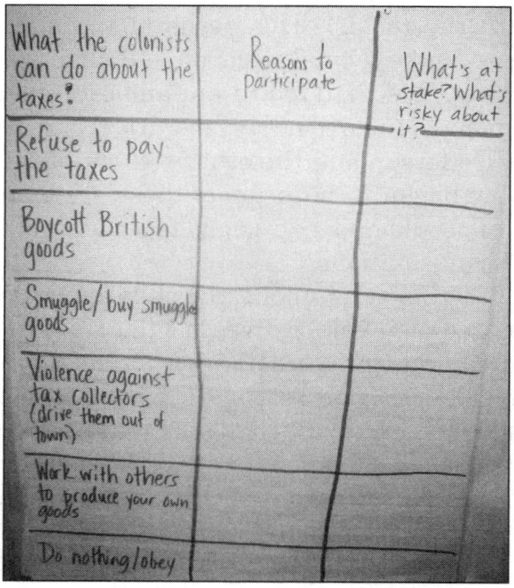

Reviewing all the different possibilities about how to react to the taxes and what to do about them led to a larger discussion about how communities and individuals can show disagreement with their governments. What means of power does the common person have? This ended up being quite a heated discussion, with some arguing (always from the perspective of their Colonial characters) to stand up to the British and resist. Others offered more moderate solutions. At the conclusion of their discussion, despite their differences, the whole class agreed that when people come together to accomplish a goal, powerful outcomes can result.

Throughout the time the children were immersed in studying taxation and creating their Colonial characters, they were also involved in book clubs, each of which was reading historical fiction about the revolutionary period. In this way literacy work was incorporated into the project so that the children could work on their literacy skills while also gaining additional contexts for their growing understandings about the colonists and their lives.

In the course of the study Martha found additional ways to foster the children's literacy development. She read a lot of nonfiction literature to the group—about the tarring and feathering of tax collectors, the Sons of Liberty, and some specific incidents that happened in Boston and New York and the colonists' reactions to those incidents. And a lot of writing was done in response to the literature. As a concluding activity to the project, for example, Martha asked the class to write about the benefits of being loyalists and patriots and then to decide whether or not to be a loyalist (stay on the side of King George) or be a patriot (go with the rebels). This assignment culminated with the children having to make a final decision—to sign the Declaration of Independence or not. They had to present and explain their decision to the group through a persuasive essay, a political cartoon, a poster, or a letter to Thomas Jefferson and the other writers of the Declaration of Independence. The bigger implication of these assignments, of course, was how groups of people make decisions together, how people respectfully discuss differing opinions.

After completing the assignment, the children, all in their Colonial characters, presented their perspectives at a final town meeting, concluding with their announcement of whether or not they would sign the Declaration of Independence. Their responses demonstrate not only a grasp of the different perspectives that led people to take different stances on the issues, but also a sense of how to address an audience to convince them of an idea. Here are a few of the children's written responses that Martha shared with me, from those who sided with the loyalists:

Dear Thomas Jefferson,

I am a black slave. In the Declaration of Independence it says that all men are created equal, but that doesn't apply for black people. All of you Patriots don't want to be slaves to the British so why would I still want to be a slave to you people? This is unfair!

Patriots, Rebels, Navy, Slaves . . . Ahh, Loyalist

Why be a Loyalist you ask? Well, many reasons, but the best of all, we will still have protection from the strongest army in the world, "the British Navy." If we stay Loyalists, we will still be protected by the Navy. The Navy will protect us from anybody who's against us or turns against us. They can protect us so that we will always be safe and not in danger. So yes, we should stay with the British so that we will always be safe.

And then there were others who advocated joining the rebels. These children, after making their presentations, used a long feather pen dipped in ink to sign a mock copy of the Declaration of Independence. Here are a few examples of the perspectives of those who advocated being a rebel:

Be a Rebel

The bloody British do not give us a chance to be free. We have to do what they want us to do for them. Now do you want to live your life like that? I want freedom from the bloody British. . . .

Enough!

I have had enough of being ruled by the British. We have had to pay taxes and the British have come to New York and have slept in our homes and our beds, making us sleep on the cold floor. We have had to pay so much money for the things we need that now many of us are poor. These are the reasons I am going to sign the Declaration of Independence. We should all sign the Declaration of Independence and then go to war. We need to do this now!

Irrespective of the decision each child made, they all used evidence and examples to present their ideas in persuasive ways that took into account the perspectives of their characters as well as the audience to whom they were presenting. This evidence of the children's learning confirmed for Martha that her goals for the project had been realized: The children understood how life in the colonies was experienced by many different kinds of people and how the events of the American Revolution shaped multiple perspectives on the situation.

And thus the study came to an end. Originally intended to take about 6 weeks, because of the constraints of the school calendar, the way the experiences sustained children's interests, and the need Martha identified at different times during the study to extend activities to enhance the children's understandings, it ended up stretching over 14 weeks. Martha was especially pleased that the work the children had done together helped them to understand some of the complexities of living in a democracy:

> It is easy for us all to look at a situation and judge and say "oh that's bad." I think this study has helped the kids go beyond that and to think about what may be a person's reasons for what they do. For example, during the study one of the colonial characters had a brother who became a tax collector because he couldn't get any other work. This brought home the point. It fits with the mission statement of the Bronx New School—that we are all about being in a community and understanding and respecting others' perspectives. This is what being a citizen in a democracy is all about. (National Center for Restructuring Education, Schools, and Teaching, 2006, n.p.)

TEACHING STRATEGIES TO SUPPORT CRITICAL THINKING

Throughout this study, Martha used a variety of teaching strategies. Some that stand out as being especially effective do so because of the manner in which she facilitated the children's learning and nurtured a feeling of community in the class by creating an atmosphere of safety and trust, the way she focused explicitly on skill and content knowledge in the context of engaging activities, and the approach she used to assessment—to inform and shape her teaching.

Facilitating Learning and Nurturing Community

As Martha worked with the children individually and in groups, she acted as a facilitator of their learning. Because she knew the content of her study well, she was able to design interesting activities that engaged her students in active experiences. Through dramatic play she helped them to understand that the process of making decisions in complex situations requires taking in the perspectives of other people. Martha explains:

> One thing I learned from this study is that this idea of playing to-gether—setting up dramatic play—is really effective for 5th graders. It is something that at first seems very young, something you would do in the first or second grade. But it turned out to be really effec-tive. It helped the kids get really involved and to get into the study in ways that just sitting down and saying "Ok, now we're going to read the Declaration of Independence and we're going to think about what it means and we're going to think about the people who were there" don't do. Actually pretending we were there helped them to want to do this work. The kids really got into their characters. This was dramatic play for older kids. And, just like with younger children, it is a really powerful way for them to learn. (National Center for Restructuring Education, Schools, and Teaching, 2006, n.p.)

Through the experiences of the town meetings, a sense of commu-nity and camaraderie grew in Martha's classroom. Martha assisted the development of this sense by making sure that the atmosphere felt safe enough for the children to share their ideas together in small groups, in pairs, and at whole-class meetings. All this contributed to making the learning feel easier and more fun.

Focusing Explicit Attention to Skills and Content in the Context of Engaging Activities

In the course of the study, Martha also made sure to help the chil-dren learn how to acquire information, view it from a variety of perspec-tives, weigh evidence to make judgments, form their own opinions, find their own answers to their questions, and then go on to generate still other questions. She assisted them throughout by asking lots of ques-tions, reflecting back to them what she heard them say, helping them clarify what they wanted to say, and probing to extend their thinking. She avoided asking right/wrong-answer questions, focusing instead on the logic of children's ideas. She often commented on effective strate-gies that she noticed the children using so that the whole class could be exposed to the benefit of what worked. She helped the children make connections to other things that had happened or that they had read, always checking in with them to make sure they understood. She gave clear directions so that everyone knew what to do, what came next, and what was expected.

Assessing to Inform and Shape Instruction

What helped Martha do all this was that she treated her teaching as a "cycle of inquiry" (see Figure 6.4). She continually assessed students' actions and work to ascertain what they knew and understood, what misconceptions they had, what skills they had acquired, and what skills they needed to work on. She used the information gained from her inquiries about her students to shape the curriculum and inform her instruction.

Her original curriculum plan was thus only a draft. The curriculum evolved based on her exploration of the students' needs, questions, and interests. As she reflected on and analyzed the information about her students that she was accumulating, she continually adjusted her plans. An example of this process can be found toward the end of the study when Martha felt that the children were only seeing one side of the story of what the British were doing. Although they had done a lot of reflective writing in their notebooks about whether to go to war, the reasons to go to war, and the kinds of egregious things the British were doing, no one was saying, "There's a *reason* the British were doing these things." That was why Martha added the assignment (explained earlier) to write about the reasons why people might choose to be a loyalist or a rebel.

To guide her teaching throughout the study, Martha used many different kinds of evidence, both informal and formal. Informal assessments involved observing and recording the work of individual

FIGURE 6.4. Teaching as a "Cycle of Inquiry"

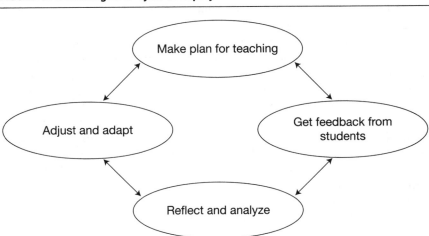

students as well as documenting whole-class discussions on charts. Keeping track of the questions students asked and the comments they made not only helped her to understand how individual students were processing their learning but also enabled her to "take the pulse" of the whole class. In addition, she learned about the children's developing knowledge through meetings with them and through presentations they made to each other, their families, and other classes.

Formal assessments included a variety of assignments that students completed as part of their projects. These called on the children to explore issues and demonstrate what they knew in a range of ways: written pieces in different genres, oral presentations, book reports, posters, and cartoons. Martha used these assignments to help keep students "on task" as well as to see whether students were ready to move on to their next challenge.

One of the benefits of having students present things in multiple ways is that through different modalities they are able to use their different skills to demonstrate what they know. Allowing for a variety of ways for children to express what they know and can do was helpful to all children in Martha's class. But its impact on one child, Etan, stood out especially. Although he was a struggling reader, one would never know it when he was involved in dramatic work. In that medium he acted confidently and convincingly. And so it made sense that, for his final project, Etan chose to present a speech to the class. Unencumbered by his struggle with the written word, his presentation was absolutely riveting. Spoken in a dialect that sounded like one of long ago, he made a convincing and moving argument about why his character chose to be a rebel. It demonstrated the wealth of information he had learned about Colonial America and its history. When Martha and I reflected on his presentation, we both agreed that without the opportunity to give a dramatic speech for his culminating assessment, Etan most likely would not have been able to reveal his understandings in as great a depth as he was able to do that day.

Martha was pleased not only by the demonstration of Etan's understanding, but also by the work of everyone in the class. As she assessed their learning at the conclusion of the study, she reflected on how the children made connections between what they learned from this project and what they had learned in past studies about how the American government currently works.

At one point, it was very cool, we were talking about Parliament and how Parliament was structured, and the kids went back in their notebook to the beginning of the year when we were doing an election study and talking about the branches of government in the United States and they were doing some comparing. . . . They all had their notebooks right there and they all went back and said, "Look, remember, we talked about who could vote." And everyone went back to their notebook and looked at that, and we were looking back and forth [from the past study to the current one]. That was surprising to me and I was quite pleased that they were able to make connections all the way back to September. (National Center for Restructuring Education, Schools, and Teaching, 2006, n.p.)

TEACHING AS A CYCLE OF INQUIRY

This study of Martha's curriculum to foster critical thinking highlights a teacher who is continually inquiring about her practice and using what she learns from her inquiries to deepen, develop, and refine her work. It demonstrates how Martha adjusted, adapted and expanded her initial plans in order to meet her students' needs. Informed by informal as well as formal assessments of her students' learning, Martha used the information she gained about what the children could do to push them to think critically and to solidify their understandings. In this way she modeled the kind of learning she wanted her students to engage in: generating questions, investigating and analyzing them, and then using the understandings gained through the investigation to shape the next steps of the learning process. Invariably this process leads to the awakening of still more questions to pursue. It demonstrates that teaching, like learning, is a cycle of inquiry that is generative and need never have an end.

CHAPTER 7

A Community of Care: Teaching the Whole Child

Many people think of curriculum as simply the activities teachers and students do in different subject areas and time blocks. In the preceding chapters, I have tried to make visible curricula that go beyond that notion. In images of well-organized, richly provisioned classrooms that offer interesting and meaningful real-world experiences, I have described teaching that leads learners toward mastery of critical skills and knowledge, supports the development of in-depth understanding, makes connections between ideas, and nurtures a critical stance toward learning. To me, this is the kind of curriculum that "teaches the way children learn."

But these elements are only part of the story. In a school that teaches the way children learn, curriculum has additional layers that add to its complexity. It also includes the learning opportunities that arise during other parts of classroom and school life—daily school routines (such as lunch and recess), the transitions that take place between one activity and another, the interactions children have with each other (individually and in groups), and even the way the school environment is set up. In this chapter I discuss these elements of teaching—what I call a "curriculum of care."

I have always felt strongly that the quality of the relationships people have with each other—the way minute-by-minute interactions are affected by the tone of a voice, the choice of a person's words, facial expressions, or other body language and whether or not a sense of respect, caring, and generosity are conveyed—play an important role in learning. Now there is brain research to confirm this (Bransford, Brown, & Cocking, 1999; Shonkoff & Phillips, 2000; Siegel, 2001). Relationships are especially key in learning environments for young children, whose identities are still newly in the making. Each exchange between a child and an adult can help nurture that child's well-being and sense of self-efficacy. Or it can undermine these critical underpinnings of personhood, ultimately getting in the way of the self-confidence needed to take charge of one's own learning and life.

Children need to be in caring communities to develop the sense of self-worth necessary to take the risks that are involved in real learning. In the same way that they need explicit attention to skills and content knowledge in meaningful contexts to effectively learn academics, children also need explicit support for their social and emotional development by being in a context of safety, trust, and care (Bredekamp & Copple, 1997; Noddings, 1984, 1992, 2002). But it is difficult for teachers to provide this context all by themselves in their classrooms. Support is also needed from the entire school community.

The Bronx New School, from its beginnings, has tried to provide this kind of support. Created to pay attention to the whole child (social/ emotional as well as academic development) and to foster respectful, equitable, and democratic relationships among all members of the school community, the school's Bill of Community Responsibilities and Rights, developed many years ago, makes evident the commitment to these ideals. Displayed in the front corridor of the school's current building, it reads:

> We, the BNS community, composed of parents, students, principal, teachers, paraprofessionals, secretaries, aides, security guards, lunch workers, custodians, and bus drivers, are working to create an atmosphere where learning and respect are held in the highest esteem. Toward that end, we have agreed to uphold the following:
>
> 1. We are responsible for our own learning, and for allowing others to learn. **We have the right to learn.**
> 2. We are responsible and accountable for our actions. **We have the right to learn from our mistakes.**
> 3. We have the responsibility to respect each other's culture. **We have the right to have our differences respected.**
> 4. We have a responsibility to speak at an appropriate time and in a manner such that people will want to listen. **We have the right to express our feelings and opinions.**
> 5. We have a responsibility to listen. **We have the right to be heard.**
> 6. We have a responsibility to act in a safe way. **We have the right to feel safe.**
> 7. We have a responsibility to respect school materials and other people's property. **We have the right to have our belongings respected.**

This Bill of Community Responsibilities and Rights provides the foundation for a schoolwide curriculum of care. It is manifested in the respectful and educative manner that people in the school communicate with each other, the collaborative approach people use to discipline and solve problems, the caring ways that adults connect to children and make sure each is well known, the structures and rituals that are designed to nurture all aspects of children's development, and the efforts to foster a sense of community within the school as well as a sense of responsibility to those in the larger world.

In this chapter I share images of these different elements of a curriculum of care.

CARING AND CAREFUL LANGUAGE

Adults in the Bronx New School consciously use language to educate. They choose their words carefully and strategically. For example, when responding to children's problematic behaviors, rather than berating or blaming, teachers comment in ways that help children understand what they have done that is helpful or what can be done to change what is unacceptable. During reading time in the kindergarten, for instance, comments like the following can be heard:

> 1, 2, 3, eyes and ears on me. Does anyone know why I might be stopping the whole class from reading? It is too loud in here for everyone to be able to do their best reading. Quiet, please.

> You know what? People are saying really important things but they don't get heard because people aren't listening to each other. It is Jose's turn to speak now. Let's show respect to Jose by giving him our full attention.

Comments like these give guidance to children for how to achieve the cooperative atmosphere teachers want to establish. It is an atmosphere that helps children think about others as well as themselves. Another example is the response given to Rachel after she made a flippant comment of "Oh, that's easy" in a class meeting, after the teacher had just completed giving out some complicated instructions to the whole group. "It might be easy for you, Rachel," said the teacher, " but not everyone might find it quite so easy."

Comments that direct children to think about how their actions and words might affect others are reinforced throughout the day. At a class meeting a teacher can be overheard saying, "Use a big voice please. Make it easy for the listeners." Or, as children lined up to leave their classroom for a walk through the halls to the art room, a teacher reminded them, "Remember, other people are in their classes working. Let's keep our voices low as we walk through the halls so that we don't disturb them."

Consciously emphasizing the positive, teachers are frequently heard commenting on the things that children do well. In different classrooms, at different times during the day, teachers offer praise and encouragement. They do this in ways that avoid evaluative words, emphasizing instead the "what" or the " how" to try to make the comments a guide: "How helpful you were to each other at work time!" or "You guys did such interesting things together!" Because we all tend to see ourselves through the eyes of others, this kind of feedback to children helps build their self-esteem.

Teachers also try to frame things in the positive, even when problems do occur. They try to state what needs to be done in positive terms, emphasizing *what* to do rather than what *not* to do. For example, "Walk please" rather than "Don't run"; or "Put the blocks on the shelf when you're done" rather than "Don't leave blocks all over the floor."

When addressing issues of behavior, teachers also try to speak to the behavior of the child, not to the child's overall character. This applies to positive as well as negative situations. How much more educative it is to say to a child, "It was so helpful when you and Janine stacked all the papers and put them on the shelf" rather than, "You and Janine are such good girls!" Framing comments in this way gives children a guide for their future actions.

Another aspect of communicating care is empathizing with children's feelings. This can be heard at the Bronx New School in statements like "I know it is hard to wait, but everyone needs to have a turn." Empathy can also be combined with language aimed at redirecting unacceptable behavior. For example, when a child is hitting in anger, a teacher may stop him or her and say, "I can see that you are very angry. You need to tell Davre how you feel with words, not with hitting." Teachers also demonstrate empathy by trying to really listen to what children have to say. They continually invite children to express their feelings.

Choices are offered to children whenever possible. In the same way that children in Ronnie's class were given the option to decide in what order to conduct the morning meeting, when teachers offer children choices during the day—such as asking them to choose which of two books they would like to read or whether they would like apples or oranges for snack—a sense of ownership and investment in the class develops. When it is not possible for teachers to give children a choice, it helps if teachers can explain why, rather than asserting their authority just because they are the teachers. For example, "You need to clean up now because it is time for us to go home."

And finally, when teachers' own frustrations overwhelm, an effort is made not to lose their tempers, be sarcastic, or use evaluative terms such as *bad, good,* and so on. Unlike some teachers I have seen in other schools, whose frustration and anger has led them to say things like, "OK, go ahead and act like this; I get paid regardless of what you do" (really, I have heard this!), teachers who teach a curriculum of care try to harness their frustration into more productive language. They express their feelings, but in a way that doesn't berate those entrusted to their care: "When you don't cooperate, it really upsets me and the other children. We really need you to try to work together with the group."

Out of a belief that motivation is most powerful when it comes from within, not without, teachers also avoid stickers, candy, and other material rewards. Rather, they try to motivate children to want to do what is best for their own learning and for the group. To do this they work to create an atmosphere where everyone feels equally valued and safe. Thus children are not singled out in front of the class as a result of their negative *or* positive behavior; they are not given coveted jobs as a reward for doing something well; teachers do not compare children against each other, display the work of only the more academically successful, or favor the children of parents who are active in the school over those whose parents are not.

Instead, educators at the Bronx New School try to achieve order, discipline, and positive behaviors by basing their actions on an understanding of children's development. They try to build on children's strengths, make them feel good about themselves, and trust them to do the right thing. Out of a belief that children inherently want to do the right thing when they are trusted, respected, and have a sense of belonging, they give them as much freedom as possible and make only rules that are necessary.

DISCIPLINE AND PROBLEM SOLVING

Meetings with individuals, with families, with small groups, with classes, and with the whole school are one of the main strategies relied on at the Bronx New School to resolve discipline issues. A problem-solving rather than adversarial perspective is used. It calls on everyone to try to mediate disputes rather than win by blaming or proving others wrong. This way of thinking requires a big change—for those trying to help resolve the conflict as well as those directly involved in the conflict. It entails thinking in terms more complex and multifaceted than "we and they, good and bad, bigger and smaller, more and less, friend and enemy, winner and loser."

Problems are tackled by encouraging children to consult with each other and work together to figure things out rather than only relying on adults as the sole authorities who have all the answers. In Martha's room, for example, I noticed the message shown in Figure 7.1 posted on the wall. This message of self-reliance is reinforced in other ways as well. For example, when Damion came to Martha with a problem he was having, she did not immediately offer a solution but instead responded: "Rosha and Malik had that problem too. Why don't you ask them about what they did? Talk about it together and then you decide."

Another example of problem solving that I noticed in Martha's class is how her group addressed a dilemma of pencils disappearing from the writing area. (To maintain an atmosphere of equality in the school, each classroom at the Bronx New School has a set of common supplies rather than each child being asked to bring in his or her own. This is done to avoid situations where some children may have more or better supplies of pencils or markers than others.) To discuss what to do about the missing pencils, Martha called a class meeting. After discussing the problem, they generated a variety of suggestions about what to do: Have somebody check the pencils at the end of each day; tape each person's name on one pencil and only use your own; put a dot on each class-owned pencil so no one will take one home by mistake; count the pencils every morning and afternoon. The class voted on which suggestion to try and then put the plan that won the most votes into action. And it worked! Right away, pencils stopped disappearing.

FIGURE 7.1. See 3 Before Me! sign

For such a "talking things through" approach to succeed, it needs to start in the very first days of school. That way it becomes part of the school's culture. This is what we did in the early years of the Bronx New School when I was the director. I used to lead an all-school meeting at the beginning of each year to generate rules to which we would hold ourselves accountable. As the children offered their suggestions, I wrote them down on big chart paper. Each rule was discussed, debated, revised, and finally agreed upon. Here is an example of the rules that were generated at the beginning of one school year:

- No running
- No fighting
- If you have a problem: (1)Talk about it; (2) Get an adult to help you
- No hitting, spitting, slapping, cursing, biting, pulling hair, kicking, pushing, teasing, or climbing on the walls
- No gum, candy, soda, or glass bottles
- No stealing
- No leaving the room without telling the teacher
- RESPECT EACH OTHER!
- LISTEN TO EACH OTHER!
- THIS IS A NONVIOLENT ZONE

In that same meeting the children also made rules for the bus. These too were written down and displayed on charts posted on the school walls:

- Wear seat belts
- Don't get out of your seats
- No flipping, jumping, or standing on the seats
- No garbage on the seats or floors
- No kicking
- No screaming, cursing, or bad language
- NO FIGHTING!

Note the words that are in capitals. This was the children's idea to add emphasis—as was the level of detail spelled out in the rules. However, sometimes the level of detail needed to be elaborated even further to help children understand not only what was not acceptable but, also, what strategies they could use instead. My notes from those times document how the children elaborated on the school rules to give greater specificity. For example, to the rule "No hitting or hitting back," the children added "If someone does something to you that you don't like, tell that person with words to stop. If that doesn't work, tell a grown-up. Say what it is that you don't like, rather than calling that person names."

If these more elaborated rules were still broken, which they inevitably were, then children would be given consequences for their actions that were educative rather than punitive. For example, rather than making a child sit on the bench in the park for the entire recess because of something he or she did wrong earlier in the morning, we would have that child sit out for only a couple of minutes immediately after the incident happened to think about what he or she did until the child came up with two things that he or she could have done differently. After this was discussed with an adult and, perhaps, with others who were involved in the problematic situation, we would allow the child to get back into the activities. How much more educative this way of handling a discipline problem is than simply punishing the child by withholding participation in fun or meaningful activities without asking the child to think and problem-solve about what it was that he or she did wrong!

The overriding message of this approach to rules and their consequences is to be respectful to others. And children, indeed, can get that message! They learn that the words we use and the ways we treat each other make a difference in the quality of our lives.

The language of care exemplified above can do much to keep discipline problems at bay. But while it can become second nature to use with a bit of thought and attention, just as easily, educators can fall back on disciplining methods that may have been used with us when we were small—yelling, name-calling, punishments. These behaviors can come so naturally that we often don't even realize what we are doing. With practice, however, it is possible to develop a language for discipline that can help children build their own inner controls, good feelings about themselves, and their capacities to care about other people. This kind of disciplining is based on guiding rather than controlling behavior. It can be accomplished in a school without line-ups, bullhorns, rows of desks, suspensions, detentions, sending children to the principal's office, or making them write "I will not run in the lunchroom" 100 times when rules are broken. When educators guide rather than try to control behavior, fewer infractions of the rules result; and even the majority of those remaining can be handled effectively through dialogue and empathic support.

I do not mean to imply that creating a school atmosphere of dialogue, democracy, and respect is a task that is easy, especially when children are accustomed to receiving harsh punishments and material rewards. But when old ways are broken and new norms of respect, courtesy, and nonjudgmental guidance are established, children feel accepted and loved, which, in turn, earns their cooperation and trust. Experiencing relationships in such a school culture is, I believe, as deep and profound a lesson in social studies as any person could learn anywhere.

MAKING CONNECTIONS

In a school that teaches the way children learn, it is the responsibility of all adults to care for all the children. The office secretaries, the food service people, the bus drivers, and the security guard all see it as part of their job. Here are a few images from the Bronx New School.

During recess the security guard at the front desk stands outside in the play street with the teachers, overseeing what the children are doing, intervening with them when needed. In the early years of the school, the security guard also read with children during the day. Struggling readers, who needed extra time and support from an adult, could frequently be found sitting with him at his desk reading aloud to him and discussing what they had read. A few pointers about how to assist emerging readers (offered to him by the reading resource teacher) went a long way toward boosting his effectiveness with this task.

Another image: At the end of the day the bus driver, rather than waiting in his bus for the children on his route, comes into the kindergarten classroom to pick them up. The children rush to give him hugs as he enters the room.

And still another: In the school office, one of the aides comes in to tell the secretary that although Paul, the school's current principal, assigned her to watch over Alex to keep him from fighting, she sensed he was on the verge of an altercation and so she brought him to the office to be safe. Alex's teacher comes in soon afterward to check on him and explain what happened. Everyone consults and decides that Alex should spend a few more moments in the office to calm himself down before reentering the classroom.

To me, this scene in the school office serves as a metaphor for all the others, depicting a community of care. The tiny room, bustling with activity, houses not only the principal and the school secretary, but also the parent coordinator and several office assistants, who are responsible for myriad tasks. In contrast to traditional images of the principal's office, where children are sent when they have been "bad," this is a friendly place to which children can come when seeking support or advice or simply a change of pace from the classroom.

This atmosphere was established in the early days of the school. It was to the office that children came with their problems or disagreements, with accomplishments to share, or to merely give and get a friendly hello. Children also came when they needed to make a phone call home or to lie down on a cot when they did not feel well. They were cared for by any available adult, who did so without regard for distinctions of rank. Any one of us could be observed resolving a conflict, bandaging a cut, or wiping away tears.

In response, the children seemed to know they could get what they needed from *someone, somewhere,* in the school. If they had difficulty connecting with their classroom teacher, they knew there were other adults with whom they could. This sense of safety and trust permeating the atmosphere of the school enabled children to confide in school personnel so that they could get help dealing with the challenges and troubles of their lives. I remember the day that I was chatting with Keisha in the library when she confided to me that she had been sexually abused. And there was the time when Kamali revealed to one of the school aides how frightened he was when his parents fought in front of him, when Lamar told the assistant teacher in his classroom how he "got beat" for wetting the bed, and when Nina confided in the school secretary that she saw her neighbor hold a gun to his wife's head during an argument. These kinds of incidents, which, sadly, are not uncommon occurrences in many communities, affect children in ways that are so deep they cannot be left at the schoolhouse door. Because of this, it is the responsibility of schools to create environments in which children feel safe enough to bring their whole selves and to disclose the truths about their lives. When this happens, they can be supported more fully. I have no doubt that doing this can literally save lives.

As of my writing of this book, an environment of safety and trust seems to be as present today at the Bronx New School as it was in the past. The grown-ups are there for the children, to connect with them and know them well in order to support them in personal as well as academic growth. Signs of the value placed on knowing children well are reflected throughout the school. For example, it is common in classrooms to see charts on the walls that share personal information about the children as well as the teachers. This one, created by the children in a class meeting, focuses on feelings:

Acts of kindness that make me feel good:

Hang out with me when I'm alone
Help me when I'm confused
Say welcome back or good morning to me
Listen to my ideas
Remind me nicely if I forget something or am not doing the
    right thing
Invite me to play and share with you

Things that people sometimes do that make me feel bad:

Fool around and cause the whole class to have problems
Make fun of me
Bother me when I ask you to stop
Make fun of my attempts at kindness (like saying you will rip
     up my card)
Threaten me

Below this chart was another with the question, "Do you need to speak to someone who made you feel bad? Tell us about it." Here a "stickie" was posted by Jack and Amman. It said, "Natalie, you wrote our name on the board when we told you not to!"

It is clear that Martha, the teacher of this class, understands that children's feelings influence their learning. She also knows that it is important for children to know about her feelings too, as evidenced by this message posted in the meeting area the first morning after returning from a school break:

Good morning! Welcome back. I don't know about you, but my
week off flew by. I hope you loved the snow and sun. Think about
a highlight you'd like to share at our go-round. (Make it something you did—not something you bought, please!) Let's have a
marvelous Monday!

Other ways that children's feelings can be taken into account in a school are evident in the corridors of the Bronx New School, where displays from different classes are set up to ensure that members of the community know about each other. On the bulletin boards one fall, each class had a photomontage, accompanied by an explanatory text. Here is an example:

Sasha's class

Hi! We are the kids in Sasha's class. One thing about our class is we
work hard on studying plants, doing our class jobs, learning frac-
tions, editing our writing, and reading our series books. We go on
lots of trips so we can study what we see there. We are able to clean
up and get ready quickly so that we have to fit in lots of things.
Another thing is that we understand each other. When people say
something we make sure they say what they mean. If we see something we don't agree with, we just don't go along with it. We try to
do something about it. You should visit our class in Room 203.

Not only are children encouraged to know others in the Bronx New School community, they are encouraged to know *themselves*, too. For example, as part of a study of Native Americans, the children in Sasha's class gave themselves names to personify something they considered to be special about them. These were displayed in their room on a "Naming Ourselves Chart." Here are some of the names the children gave to themselves: Lucky Coin, Listener, Feeling Very Safe, Soft Cheek, Red Bull, Praying for Animals, The Boy Who Cares, Spirit of the East, Thinks Before He Does it, Playful Boy, Talk Too Much, Pretending My Brother Isn't There, The Mad Eagle, Praying to the Earth, Takes Care of Things.

In addition to this evidence about how the children are encouraged to know each other and themselves, other evidence about how they are known by their teachers was revealed to me poignantly at an end-of-the-year graduation ceremony I attended one June day. Toward the end of the event, each of the teachers spoke directly to the children in their class, sharing things they had learned about them. Althea, one of the fifth-grade teachers, first told the children how proud she was of them for their hard work. Then, after reminding them that during their time at the school they had shared themselves and their spirits with each other, she talked about how what she had learned about each child gave her confidence about what was to come next in their lives. "Today marks the day of a new part of your future. I want you to know I've been listening to you." She then proceeded to tell each child what she had heard and noticed about them and what her hopes for the future were for each. Here are a few examples of what she said:

> Cora, basketball is magic in your hands. And don't forget, keep on dancing.

> Jonathan, you've always loved making people laugh. You must find a way to share your gift of laughter with the world.

> Jana, what a gentle and nurturing spirit you are. I just know you can be a wonderful artist or poet.

How affirming this demonstration of being well known and cared for must have been for the children as they prepared to move out to the world beyond their first little school.

STRUCTURES, ROUTINES, AND ACTIVITIES OF CARE

A curriculum of care requires structures to support it. At the Bronx New School, "looped" classes, all-school meetings, after-school programs, attention to the arts, class museums and celebrations, and other practices and routines are all designed to ensure that attention is paid to the whole child and that each child is cared for and well known.

Class Structures

One of the reasons that Bronx New School teachers know their children so well is that the children stay with them for 2 years. Originally, classes were made up of mixed-age groups—K/1s, 2/3s, 4/5s. Each class had children who spanned 2 years of age—the younger half of the class would be new each year and the older half of the class would remain from the previous year. The idea behind this way of organizing the class structure was to provide a wider developmental span in the class in order to support diverse learning styles, paces, and interests. Because in a mixed-age class diversity rather than uniformity is the norm, students of different strengths have a greater probability of finding peers who have similar strengths and needs. To support these different strengths and needs, teachers must be sure to provide opportunities for children to work in different ways. This increases the likelihood that children will get to learn in a manner that suits them. Also, because in mixed-age classes the range of what is considered to be normal is broader than in a single-aged class, children don't stand out as much (and get stigmatized) for being less advanced in some areas over others. Rather, they get opportunities to learn from their more advanced peers in their areas of weakness while they are also able to work ahead in areas in which they are strong. They learn by interacting with others who are at various places on the learning continuum.

In recent years at the Bronx New School, the benefits of mixed-age classes came into conflict with the pressures of tests and curriculum mandates. After a lot of discussion and heated debate, the mixed-grade structure at the school was replaced with "looping." While this structure has only one grade/age group per class, it maintains the practice of having the children stay with the same teacher for 2 years. So, for example, a second-grade teacher stays with his or her class when they move up to the third grade. When the class moves on to the fourth grade, that teacher begins working with another group of second graders, with whom he or she stays for another 2 years. This structure, while lacking the broader range of "normalcy" found in a mixed-age class (so difficult to maintain in this era of yearly mandated standards and testing), keeps the important benefit of having teachers know their students well. Teachers have the time to establish strong connections and bonds of care.

All-School Meetings

Another structure that helps to create a community of care is all-school meetings. In its founding years, the Bronx New School held weekly all-school meetings, originally known as "School Sing." Each Friday morning prior to lunch, I convened and led the gathering. Since I had been a music specialist in the early years of my teaching career, I used my guitar and all the songs I knew to create a sense of community with children and staff. Intended at first as a time when I and school aides would relieve the classroom teachers so that they could have a bit of time during the school day for planning or working on their rooms, this weekly event soon became compelling enough that the teachers found themselves staying and participating.

In addition to enjoying music together, the teachers and children at the meeting took advantage of everyone being together to share information, raise issues that were on their minds, present works in progress, or display finished projects of classroom studies. School Sing soon morphed into what we called All-School Meeting.

A few memorable presentations stand out in my memory of those All-School Meetings of the early Bronx New School days. One is when a second-grade class shared their work from a study of Egypt that they had just completed. As an outgrowth of a study on mummies, the children had learned about Egypt and made a papier-mâché topographical map of it. To present the map to the school, the class selected Kalen, a small, wiry little guy, as their spokesperson. All by himself he carried the large, unwieldy map to the front of the room and then proceeded to explain its details. Following his explanation, the children had lots of questions and comments. One child pointed out what she thought was a mistake: the Upper Nile was placed at the bottom of the map while the Lower Nile was placed at its top. No one was really quite sure why this was so. Several speculations were offered as explanation and then someone noticed that a mountain range (remember, this was a topographical map) ran parallel to the river. Perhaps the Upper Nile was the top of the mountain, the Lower Nile the bottom, someone suggested. That must be it, the group agreed; that answer made sense. Then one of the fifth graders volunteered to go to the school's library to check out this fact in the encyclopedia. On her return she confirmed that the earlier response based on the river's relationship to the mountain was correct; the group had indeed figured out the answer. Everyone was delighted by this group problem-solving experience.

Another of my favorite School Sing memories was the day the fifth-grade class presented me with a petition, on behalf of the entire student body, protesting the school's no-candy rule. The children felt this rule was unfair. They had two reasons, the first being that they saw no negligible difference between having candy (which was not allowed in the school at all) or having a piece of cake or a cookie (which was allowed) for their dessert at lunchtime; the other being that they had seen teachers eating candy during the course of the school day and felt it wasn't fair that teachers could have candy when kids could not. (In truth, there was always a box of some kind of chocolate in the right bottom-hand drawer of my desk. Frequently teachers would drop by my office during the day to have a little "pick-me-up" from that drawer.) Well aware of the teachers' trips to my office for their "fix," the children were indignant about the injustice of what they perceived to be a clear double standard. So a few fifth graders organized a petition drive and got almost all the children in the school (even the kindergartners) to sign it. When Renata, the leader of this initiative, read the petition at School Sing, it was greeted with hoots and cheers of support. Sheepishly realizing that their logic made sense, the teachers and I negotiated a new agreement with the children: Children could have candy for dessert but only at their tables during lunch; teachers would indulge their chocolate habit only during after-school hours. What a lesson in problem solving that was! Remembering it still gives me a chuckle. But the incident is actually a great example of how listening and responding to children's concerns can help them feel their power and can strengthen a community.

The Bronx New School of today continues the tradition of All-School Meetings. During these meetings, each class takes turns presenting some issue or aspect of their work. When Martha's class was doing their study of Colonial New York, for example, the children made a presentation about it at All-School Meeting. They made up a skit explaining what they were learning. The experience of explaining what they knew so that even kindergartners could understand it really helped them consolidate their knowledge.

Another particularly memorable recent All-School Meeting I witnessed was held at the culmination of a study of data collection that every class in the school was involved in. In the open meeting space on the school's second floor, all the classes posted data charts on the walls and took turns sharing with the others what they had studied, how they had collected the data, and what they had learned from it (see Figure 7.2).

FIGURE 7.2. All-school meeting

The kindergartners and first graders exhibited charts they had made for how many seeds are in a pumpkin. They also showed a variety of charts about how many letters/syllables are in different peoples' names (see Figure 7.3).

The second- and third-grade classes shared charts they had made during a study of water. They displayed maps and diagrams they had made after surveying water sources inside and outside the building. A tally chart depicted what they had found:

Water Sources

2nd floor sinks: 17	1st floor sinks: 18	
2nd floor toilets: 7	1st floor toilets: 12	
2nd water fountains: 3	1st floor water fountains: 2	

Those same classes also shared a thank you note that they had written to the school's custodian, who had taken them on a tour of the basement to show them how water enters the building pipes, the pump that brings it upstairs, and the boiler that heats it up (see Figure 7.4.).

The fourth and fifth graders presented data from their study of people living in their homes. They had counted the number of people in their homes, the number of those who were home during the day, and the number of those who went out to work. These children shared the bar and line graphs they had made that were based on this data.

FIGURE 7.3. Letters in name chart

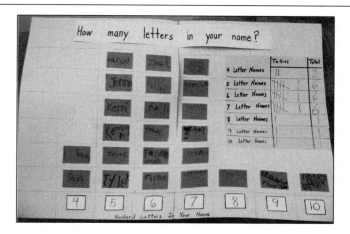

FIGURE 7.4. Water study letter

November 19, 2005

Dear Russell,
    How are you doing?
Thank you for taking us to
the basement! I learned a lot
about how water travels in our
school. I really appreciate it.
Thank you for taking your busy
day off to show us around the
basement. I really liked visiting
the basement!
    I learned how water comes
into our school. I also learned
how the water gets heated. I
learned where the water goes when it
gets dirty and I learned where the
water comes from and how the water
gets to evrey class in the school.
    How do you remember what are all
the pipes for? Do all buildings have a
basement? How does it feel to know
all that stuff about the basement?
See you next time!

From this celebration of their work the children learned from and with each other. Doing this strengthened their sense of community. Other school structures strengthen it as well.

Other Structures

In recognition of the need for working families to have a safe and caring place for their children after school, an after-school program sponsored by a local community agency is held at the Bronx New School every day. Participating children get help with their homework as well as take dance, art, and other courses.

Experiences with the arts are not limited, however, just to after-school hours. The arts are valued in the school as important opportunities to explore the world, awaken imagination, and nurture each person's sense of possibility. Throughout the school day there are classes in art, drama, dance, and music taught by school staff or practicing artists in residence. At times, the children also get exposed to the arts through performances that are brought into the school or through visits to cultural institutions, all of which are made possible by the generosity of grants.

In the early years of the school, a troupe from the New York City Ballet visited and gave a lecture/demonstration. Then the children were invited to Lincoln Center for a holiday performance of the *Nutcracker* ballet. For many of the children, who had never before been out of the few blocks' radius of their Bronx neighborhood, this was a totally awesome experience. I'll never forget the sound of their reactions ("Oooh!") as the bus pulled up that evening in front of the building and water fountain all decorated in Christmas lights at the glamorous arts complex. We were treated to dinner and a performance. What a night!

Over the years, grant funding has brought special arts projects to the school, too. In the early years, when we were cramped into the basement Sunday School corridor of the Fordham Methodist Church, we solicited and received a Molly Parness Dress Up Your Neighborhood Award from the local citizen's committee so that we could paint over the dirty walls of the basement window wells, which were the only openings we had for fresh air. The current Bronx New School has child-painted murals on both the inside and outside walls of the school (see Figure 7.5). The beauty of the surround symbolizes the care that is within.

Class Celebrations

Other rituals demonstrate care as well. All the classes, at various times during the school year, hold Museums or Celebrations at the completion of a study. To these they invite their families as well as other classes and adults in the school. In addition to the Museum for the Undersea Study described in an earlier chapter, another Museum that stands out in my mind is a "Think Big" exhibit, which culminated a third grade's study of measurement and scale. Each student crafted a model of an everyday object blown up to exact, gigantic proportions (see Figure 7.6). When they were finished the class held a Think Big exhibition, filling the classroom with giant pencils, rulers, credit cards, erasers, soda cans, frying pans, and other such items. Not only did the children learn to do proportional measurement, they really had a lot of fun.

FIGURE 7.5. Stairway mural

FIGURE 7.6. Think big

In addition to museums, classes also hold celebrations at the conclusion of a unit or project. The most popular of these, both in the past and currently, is a Writers' Celebration. When a class finishes a study, for example, when the kindergarten class completed a study of the works of Mem Fox, the children invite others to visit their classroom to view their own author-inspired stories and drawings as well as their written responses to the author's work. When Ronnie's class held their Writers' Celebration a few years ago, they even made admission tickets for their guests (see Figure 7.7).

At the event, class members sat with their open writing folders at different tables around the room. Teachers and children from other classes, along with visiting caregivers and siblings, stopped at the tables to read and discuss the children's work. Sometimes the visitors asked questions; sometimes they wrote remarks on a comment sheet included in each child's folder. Refreshments were served. The atmosphere was festive. Before guests left they wrote comments about the celebration on a note card that they placed in a basket by the door.

Lessons from Lunch

Other routines in the school that build a community of care are associated with lunch and recess. These have been carefully designed to

FIGURE 7.7. Writer's Celebration Ticket

support a sense of belonging, of trust, of safety, and of respect. Some examples: Teachers and assistants escort their classes to the lunchroom every day, settling the children at their assigned tables before leaving for their own break. Older children, acting as helpers, assist the younger ones in getting their trays or opening their packaged lunches brought from home. They also act as mediators when problems occur. The children respond positively to each other's efforts to maintain a peaceful atmosphere during lunch.

During recess, children of all ages and classes mingle together, enjoying the company of each other and the school's adults. Today's school community has a play street directly in front of the school. But in the early years of the school, we either had to walk across a busy thoroughfare to get to a park or we stayed in the lunchroom during inclement weather. A club structure was devised, which still exists today, for children to engage in various activities—cards at one table; board games at another; bracelet making, paper airplane making, cartooning, plasticine modeling at still others. In a corner of the room some older children would frequently gather around a small stereo, trying out new dance steps to the music. Another empty floor space was used for younger children, who were building constructions with large cardboard blocks. Out a side door in a narrow alleyway, still other groups of children, overseen by an adult, jumped rope, played hopscotch, and drew with colored chalk on the cement walk.

Today, an origami club offered by the school librarian (a volunteer who is over 90 years old!) also meets a few times a week during recess. These activities create a busy and happy atmosphere in which children of different ages comfortably interact with the adults and with each other. This all-school open time offers opportunities for doing interesting things with different people. It also affords school staff yet another opportunity to observe children in natural ways and to learn more about the strengths and interests of individuals. Recess reveals powerful aspects of the learning process that often get lost in classroom settings— the power of cooperative learning and self-generated work (as children select their activities and form their own groups), the independent drive for excellence that individuals possess (endlessly practicing dance steps or jump rope routines until they are perfected), children's understanding of and need for standards (collectively working out the rules of the game), the effective role of teacher as facilitator (the adults setting things up and then making themselves available to help only when needed), the love of performance (children showing each other what they can do after perfecting their dance or jump rope routine), and the desire to engage in meaningful and purposeful tasks (children choosing activities of interest and then setting their own purposes for task completion).

These "lessons from lunch/recess" (Renyi, 1992) are subsequently used by teachers as invaluable guides for expanding teaching efforts in their classrooms. They inspire teachers to focus beyond cognitive skills and curriculum content to also support children to develop positive dispositions toward learning.

RESPONSIBILITY AND RESPECT FOR THE COMMUNITY

All the activities, structures, and routines described above demonstrate how a school can go beyond just a focus on academic learning to nurture all aspects of children's development. Included in this focus on the whole child is an emphasis on being a good citizen in the community—learning to consider others within the school as well as those in the larger world. Below are a few examples of what this looks like.

Within the school, children take responsibility for many aspects of their daily lives. A sign posted on one of the classroom's walls indicates the emphasis on being a good citizen:

We are the kind of class that holds people responsible for what they do. Think before you act!

As in most schools, all classrooms have jobs, which are rotated among the students. But there are other, schoolwide jobs that help children take on a sense of community ownership and responsibility. One such job is being a tour guide for prospective students and their families. Because the Bronx New School is a school of choice (families apply and get selected through a lottery), there are frequent visits by prospective students and their families. Long ago we worked out a system that put the students in charge of a portion of these tours. One of the older classes, as part of a study they did of measurement, measured the school and made a map of it to scale. This was turned into a handout that visitors could use as their hosts showed them around. The children also answered visitors' questions before escorting them to a meeting with the principal and other adults.

Besides assuming responsibilities within the school, children and teachers reach out to the world at large to learn about social responsibility. One year a concern for the environment led the children to take on a recycling project. They decided to do two kinds of recycling: first, they collected junk materials for use in classroom projects, such as newspapers for art projects and old toy pieces and household items for scientific creations; second, they sorted the garbage in the lunchroom for recycling. One of the children brought in a video about recycling that her brother had made with other students at his high school. The whole school got involved with this project.

Other projects the children got involved in extended to the community as well. One spring the school participated in a community garden. Each class had an individual class plot—one grew a salad garden, another flowering plants; some raised sunflowers and pumpkins. All the children also contributed to the common garden in some way. They brought food garbage from the lunchroom to the garden for composting, planted morning glories to cover the garden's fencing, and built a cold frame so that the gardening season could be extended into the fall.

On one Thanksgiving a food drive for homeless people was organized. It was inspired by a visit from a neighborhood priest who runs an organization that provides housing for the homeless. He spoke to the children about the importance of according dignity to all people, no matter what their circumstances. He referred to having a home as a basic human right. After his visit the children decided to bring in donations and deliver them to shelter. The visit they made moved them so much that they wrote letters to the mayor pleading for him to give more assistance to the homeless. They also wrote poems expressing their concerns. Here is what one fifth grader wrote:

I AM HOMELESS . . .

I am
Homeless . . .
            It's lonely. When I'm homeless . . .
Each day I wait for a miracle.
No one loves you
When you're homeless . . .
If you're homeless . . .

When you're homeless . . .
You don't have
Friends.
When you're homeless . . .

When you're
Homeless . . .

        You sleep in a box.
        You wake up in the morning,
        looking for food, just anywhere
        If you're homeless . . .

        When you're homeless . . .
        In the summer.

When you're homeless . . .
The muggy weather hugs you,
but when you try to hug back
there's nothing there.
In the summer.
When you're homeless . . .

When you're homeless . . .
If you're lucky when you find food
it's usually orange peels or apple skins.
When you're homeless . . .

When you're homeless . . .
People don't care about you
You wish they did and would help.
When you're homeless . . .

When you're homeless . . .
In the Fall.
When you're homeless . . .
The leaves are scattered around you,
and you get covered.
You see kids play in the leaves with
rosy cheeks and having fun.
When you're what mean kids call a bum.
When you're homeless . . .

When you're homeless . . .
You go to sleep in your box, and
Wake up on a train to nowhere.
When you're homeless . . .

When you're homeless . . .
In the winter.
When you're homeless . . .
The cold wind covers your face,
And you wait for your turn to warm
your hands on the bonfire.
In the winter.
When you're homeless . . .

When you're homeless . . .
That is what happens . . .
When you're homeless . . .

(This poem was written by Rebecca Einbender Nole and is reprinted here with her permission.)

PLACING CARE AT THE CENTER OF EDUCATIONAL PRACTICE

The philosopher Nel Noddings (1984, 1992, 2002) conceptualizes caring as the development of enduring, reciprocal, and responsive relationships. She theorizes that teachers can teach care through modeling, practice, dialogue, confirmation, and most of all, knowing students well. At the Bronx New School an ethic of care is at the center of all educational practices. The stories shared in this chapter demonstrate how deeply children are affected by the ways adults pay attention to them, make connections with them, and help them make connections with the world. Children's comments at interviews I conducted with several classes give testimony to this fact:

> It is small here. Everyone knows each other and it feels like home.

> The whole school is like one big family. It's like having a massive amount of brother and sisters. My teachers are like second moms or dads.

> The activities are interesting and fun and we are learning at the same time.

> Whenever we do something, everyone has an opinion and no one is ignored.

> The teachers, when they read a book, they are really into it and there's never enough time to do all you want to do.

> It is special here because people help you when you're stuck.

> Every year when I leave this school, I am always sad. I just want to thank my teachers for getting me where I am.

CHAPTER 8

Culturally Relevant and Responsive Teaching

Diversity is both an opportunity and a challenge (Banks, 2006). For educators the opportunity is the potential to have students' ethnic, cultural, and language diversity enrich our lives by enabling us to see the world through others' eyes. The challenge is to respect and use students' diversity to enhance and support their learning and, ultimately, to close the racial/cultural gap in achievement as well as the ability to realize one's potential. As I see it, doing away with this gap is the responsibility of a democratic society.

Despite current concerns about the achievement gap, many approaches to teaching diverse students (many of whom have been chronically underserved in schools as well as in other aspects of life) still are based on minimal standards for achievement. In efforts to improve performance on high-stakes tests, many schools that serve diverse learners often neglect important areas of learning, adopting and mandating mass-produced curricula, constricting the focus of what gets taught to what gets tested. Some schools and districts also adopt corporate approaches to education, such as paying students and their families for good grades or school attendance. School districts in Georgia, Maryland, and New York, to name only a few, have initiated cash incentive programs (Lake, 2008). During the time I was writing this book there was even a proposal made in New York City to give children free minutes on cell phones for good test scores! Practices such as these, while no doubt appealing to some in our hypermaterialistic world, cannot possibly ensure that all children learn. While they may show short-term progress in academic achievement, I would argue that, in the long run, the long-term effects do more harm than good, ultimately fostering alienation among students, teachers, families, and communities (Hilliard, 2006). Student performance will improve only, I believe, when learning is meaningful; motivation is intrinsic; children, families, and professionals are respected and invested in the school; and pedagogy is responsive to the diverse needs and strengths of the students who are involved.

Being responsive to diversity entails developing a perspective that sees diversity as riches, not as deficits. It also involves developing an approach to teaching that uses diversity as a resource for learning. To do this, educators first need to better understand diversity. We need to deepen our understandings of the complexities of how race, ethnicity, language, social class, "abledness," gender, gender orientation, and other differences affect student learning and behavior. Based on these understandings, educators also need to ensure that all children learn and have positive relationships among and across different groups and that in these contexts, children have opportunities to discuss cross-cutting human values, develop skills for how to relate to different groups, and have safe and caring environments for their interactions (Banks, 2006; Delpit, 2006a, 2006b; Hollins, King, & Hayman, 1994; Ladson-Billings, 1994, 2005; Nieto, 1999).

Much of what I have discussed in the preceding chapters addresses these aspects of effective teaching for diverse learners. It exemplifies what Gloria Ladson-Billings (1994) has called "culturally-relevant" teaching and Geneva Gay (2000) has called "culturally responsive" teaching. Developed in response to students' understandings and experiences, the images presented show how teachers use students' strengths and differences as resources for learning. In this chapter I offer more images of culturally relevant and responsive teaching. First, I focus specifically on practices that teach *to* and *about* diversity.

TEACHING TO DIVERSITY

At the Bronx New School efforts are made to develop understanding and respect by using cultural diversity as a learning resource. This is done in everyday instances as well as through special programs and projects aimed at developing awareness of prejudice and actively countering it, celebrating the diversity of the school's children and families, and being responsive to children's cultural and language differences in all aspects of their learning. Some examples below explain how.

Confronting Our Biases

The Bronx New School community is made up of children, families, and staff from many different ethnic and racial backgrounds. A variety of skin tones, hair colors and textures, languages, and accents are apparent. Family histories are as varied as the shades of skin. Yet while the overall atmosphere of the school fosters respect for differences and support for crossing boundaries, with children of different colors and backgrounds actually "sitting together in the cafeteria" (to use the words of Beverly Daniel Tatum), prejudice inadvertently appears. "Prejudice is one of the inescapable consequences of living in a racist society. . . . [It] is like smog in the air. Sometimes it is so thick it is visible, other times it is less apparent, but always, day in and day out we are breathing it in. None of us would introduce ourselves as 'smog-breathers' (and most of us don't want to be described as prejudiced), but if we live in a smoggy place, how can we avoid breathing the air?" (Tatum, 2003, p. 6).

Throughout its history the Bronx New School community has been aware of this smog. Perhaps because people from different backgrounds have always been in such constant and close proximity in the school, awareness of prejudice has been especially keen. But the school ethos has always been to take responsibility for cleaning up that "smog"; to continually examine behavior and question if and how each person contributes to the negative messages that are so pervasive in our culture.

Celebrating the Colors of Our Skins

An incident that occurred in Sasha's third-grade class highlights how this responsibility is upheld. During recess one day, in the midst of a heated argument between two children, one made a racial slur against another, at which point a physical altercation broke out. As per usual procedures, the fight was immediately broken up, followed by admonitions to "talk with words, not with hands." One of the adults overseeing the recess then moderated a discussion between the two children to help them talk out what they were fighting about. Nevertheless, the fight caused a stir in the play street that left many of the children riled up.

When the class returned to their room after recess, their feelings were still running high. Sasha, a teacher highly attuned to his students' needs, sensed the energy in the atmosphere and, realizing the futility of trying to go on with the activity he had planned, gave the children an opportunity to talk about what had happened. As the class launched into a discussion about name-calling, he embraced the incident as a "teachable moment," using it as an opportunity to help them process their feelings and thoughts about differences. This led to a monthlong project about differences, enhanced by books Sasha brought into the classroom on race, ethnicity, gender, religion, and other aspects of differences that either bring people together or tear them apart. Central to the study were portrait painting (led by his student teacher Rachel; see Figure 8.1) and poetry writing, as Sasha described:

The study involved observing our skin closely and trying to match the tone by mixing many colors (learning that even unlikely ones such as blue were part of the mix for many children), then studying our skin again with partners and constantly revising the color mixing. The poetry came out of a study of descriptive language and much rereading of *Black Is Brown Is Tan* by Arnold Adoff (2004) and a few other anchor texts. It was the doing of this work and then the celebrating of the whole array of portraits and poems that brought forth the real learning, beyond what discussions alone could have.

My skin . . .
Is a beautiful color of sand,
Sand and the crust of pie when it just came out,
Sandy crust
And the color of peaches and creamy peanut butter on toast.

I am a cinnamon brown
A bottle of apple juice that just got made.
I am the color of a nice cardboard box
I am the color of a penny with sunshine on it

I am a tasty tan
A crispy tan
I am a hungry tan
I am a light tan
Reflections from a glass
I'm smooth as
A
Paper flat

Figure 8.1. Display titled "Sasha and Rachel's Class's Delicious Colors"

Learning About Our Differences and Similarities

In the beginning days of the Bronx New School, cultural and so-cioeconomic differences were a continual source of wariness on the part of the adults. The school district was deeply divided along racial and socioeconomic lines. Tensions ran high between the less-resourced communities in the district that were predominantly of color and the more affluent, more "White" communities. While per pupil expenditures were technically the same for all schools, the equal funding was not sufficient to address the disparities between the two communities. Differences were apparent in the condition of the buildings and their surrounds, the amount of extra resources brought in by parent associations, and student outcomes on standardized tests.

In addition to these disparities, another source of tension in the district stemmed from the fact that, like many districts in the United States, the families who attended the schools were from diverse backgrounds while the majority of teachers and administrators represented the dominant culture, namely White and middle-class. And, not surprisingly, the attitudes and norms of those in charge dominated the schools' culture. There seemed to be little awareness of the attitudes, traditions, and needs of people from different backgrounds. For example, families were often blamed by school personnel for their low attendance at school meetings instead of their realizing that a variety of reasons could be responsible—such as that there were parents who might not feel comfortable because of their language differences, who were undocumented and thus shied away from "official" places, who could not afford the bus or train fare to come to the school, or whose cultures traditionally viewed teachers with such awe and respect that ordinary people felt it was not their place to get involved.

Another factor affecting family involvement was the less-than-welcoming atmosphere that many had previously experienced in the district schools. In my own neighborhood school, for example (as mentioned in the Introduction to this book), parents were rarely allowed to visit their children's classrooms. Parent involvement was encouraged for candy sales and other fund-raising activities, but had little to do with matters of educational substance. Generally, it was a small, homogeneous group of parents who were the activists of the parents' association. They were involved in only a limited way in the school's educational issues.

This narrow view of family involvement dominated the culture of most schools and, in the early days of the Bronx New School, affected the way people thought about home-school connections. Although families from many walks of life were the creators of the school, and even though we wanted the school to be a community where all were welcomed and involved, it was difficult to shed past habits and perspectives to create new, more equitable relationships. So, early on in the school's history, to help us develop better connections, the parent coordinator organized a series of parent meetings to address issues of diversity. At one gathering that was a part of this initiative, about 30 parents sat in a circle to share their family histories. One by one we went around the circle telling others about the meanings of our names, our countries of origin (as far back as we were privileged to know), and some aspect of our culture we were most proud of. As we shared, we were amazed at the similarities we discovered among us: that people who identified themselves as "Black" came from places as diverse as Africa, the Caribbean, or the southern United States; that people with both light and dark skin shared common ancestry with Italians, Germans, and Native Americans; and that people representing all skin colors had been denied, in different ways, knowledge of their history because of various forms of discrimination. We learned how people's different cultural backgrounds shaped their attitudes toward school as well as other aspects of life. And we came to see that, despite our differences, we all had similar goals for our children. Those of us who participated in this experience came away with heightened sensitivities about differences as well as an appreciation for the commonalities we shared.

The Storytelling Project: Using Diversity as a Resource

Another example of using diversity as a resource is a storytelling project that was initiated, with support from a foundation grant, in the early years of the Bronx New School. The intent of the project was to use children's family members as learning resources by having them share and write stories about their lives. The stories were first told orally at all-school meetings. Later they were taped, transcribed, and edited into a volume that became a permanent part of the school's library (see Figure 8.2). The contributions, from grandparents, parents, other family members, and even school staff, modeled for children ways of finding out about and valuing their histories. The intention was also to inspire them, in turn, to tell and write stories of their own.

The stories shared were as diverse as the people. Parents, grandparents, aunts, and uncles came forward to tell about their lives. Stories about food (southern, Jewish, African, Irish, and Asian), about childhood experiences, about ancestors' legends, about memories of the babies who were now the school's students—all provoked emotional expressions ranging from hilarity to empathy, sadness, and sometimes tenderness that touched everyone's hearts.

FIGURE 8.2. Family stories book cover

Family Portraits:
Stories in the Oral
Tradition

One story that was born from this project was first told at School Sing by an African American grandmother who was raising two children in the school:

Let me tell you about Harlem. When I was a little girl I didn't like Harlem too much. After my mother died I was raised in Philadelphia with my grandmother. But Daddy lived in New York, so I went back and forth.

Summer months I was here in New York with Daddy. Daddy was a good-looking man. He was a woman's man. He had a little car and on Saturdays we went down on 116th Street to the market to get the chicken and other food for Sunday. On Saturdays, we got all dressed up. Well, you got dressed up every day and you never saw anybody looking dirty or ragged on this special day.

Thursdays were good days too when I grew to be in my teens. Pot Handler's Holiday, they called it. When people who slept in as domestics were off on Thursdays, everybody would get really dressed and dapper. The men had spats, walking sticks, nice gloves. Very "Dapper Dans" they were. And their shoes shined like new money. And the ladies wore their little hats and their tailor made suits. The children wore little black patent leather shoes and great big ribbon sashes and ribbons in their hair. We'd all go down on Seventh Avenue walking. The trees were lined up on Seventh Avenue on both sides of the street. There was no garbage on Thursdays on Seventh Avenue. It was always like a dream. And the people were friendly. (Morrison, 1991, p. 34)

Hearing this story at an all-school meeting triggered a flood of stories from the children about their own experiences and a discussion about similarities and differences. From this experience, the children took away an appreciation for how history is the story of people's lives.

Family storytelling can be an effective tool for realizing a cultur- ally relevant and responsive curriculum. Grounded in the experiences of community members from different racial, ethnic, linguistic, and socioeconomic backgrounds, the stories demonstrate and promote re- spect for the richness of our lives' diversity. As children, their fami- lies, and school staff share together and reveal details of their histories that are generally known only by family and friends, they gain deeper understandings about and appreciation for each other. The everyday occurrences of known people's lives become valuable resources of his- tory and culture, providing an authentic foundation for a multicultural curriculum.

Using stories in this way supports a school's commitment to achiev- ing high standards for all members of the community. In particular, it supports literacy development in a culturally responsive way—by pro- viding meaningful, purposeful contexts for writing and by valuing the multiple literacies of the children and their families.

Respecting Our Language Differences

An indicator of a school that values diversity is that it respects the language diversity of its children and families. Rather than language differences being viewed as a problem, they are viewed as a resource as well as a right. This includes the right to use dialect variation as well as second or more languages. At the Bronx New School this right has traditionally been recognized by supporting children's efforts to "code- switch" between the language of their home (their own vernacular) and Standard English. Instead of correcting children for their "mistakes" and labeling their home language as wrong or inferior, teachers put into practice what many linguists have long argued for: that students who speak in speech patterns other than Standard English are gen- erally writing or speaking correctly in the language patterns of their home and their community (Delpit, 2002; Perry & Delpit, 1998; Rich- ardson, 2003; Rickford, 1999; Smitherman, 1977; Troutman, 1999). In recognition of this, teachers use the children's diverse language variet- ies, drawing on the linguistic knowledge that they bring to school, to help them recognize the grammatical differences between home speech and school speech. The goal is to develop the tools they need to choose the most appropriate language style in their speaking and writing for the time, place, audience, or purpose.

For example, teachers might make a chart that lists, on one side, the way children say something in their home language (informal language) and lists, on the other side, the way that same thing would be written in a book (formal language). The chart could deal with noun-verb agreement, possessive patterns, or past-tense endings—common issues for those whose home language is not Standard English. Such a chart could look like this one created by Rebecca Wheeler and Rachel Swords (2006, p. 115):

Informal English	Formal English
I am tall.	I am tall.
You is tall.	You are tall.
Jaden is tall.	Jaden is tall.
We is tall.	We are tall.
You is tall.	You are tall.
They is tall.	They are tall.

This approach to learning about Standard English and how it differs from other language variations is called *contrastive analysis*. Rather than being simply corrective and assuming that there is only one right way to speak and write, it acknowledges the validity of multiple ways to convey ideas. Teachers who have used this approach have had great success in eliminating the racial achievement gap in their classrooms (Wheeler & Swords, 2006). Not only does this approach improve children's writing and performance on standardized tests, it also promotes a positive climate by honoring children's cultures and backgrounds and affirming their language differences as assets. Welcoming children's languages and cultures into the classroom in this way invites the whole child into the school. And taking the whole child into consideration—his or her feelings, experiences, background, culture—is crucial to academic success (Association for Supervision and Curriculum Development, 2007; Bransford et al., 2000).

Early in the Bronx New School's history, when children were first introduced to the process writing approach, they were encouraged to draft in their own vernaculars. We found that when they did not have to concentrate initially on correct grammar, they were able to express their ideas more freely. After they got comfortable exploring their thoughts and ideas in their own modes of discourse, we found that the children were ready and willing to focus on how to express themselves in the conventional ways of Standard English—what we called "what words would look like if you were to read them in most books."

Bolstered by the recognition that they are not linguistically impoverished but, rather, positively adept at multiple literacies, children with linguistic differences (whether they speak Spanish or Chinese or vernacular Black English) who are treated in this way learn to master the discourse patterns of what Lisa Delpit (2006b) calls "the culture of power." This helps them not only to master what is needed for school success but also to feel good about who they are and where they come from.

TEACHING ABOUT DIVERSITY

In addition to using diversity as a resource in teaching, a culturally relevant and responsive school uses every opportunity to learn about the perspectives and contributions of the diverse populations in our human community.

Of course, everyone takes advantage of holidays such as Columbus Day and Martin Luther King Jr.'s birthday to celebrate diversity. These are great opportunities to honor important people and traditions in our collective history. And then there is Black History Month, Hispanic American Day, Chinese New Year, and other observances that have made their way into the consciousness of our society. These too can be viewed as opportunities to recognize differences. But respect for diversity needs to take place more than one day or one month during the year. It needs to involve something much deeper—a consciousness about different perspectives that is infused throughout every element of school life. A few examples below offer images of what I mean.

Holidays

Holidays are a common vehicle in schools to take note of differences among us. Through discussion of our different religions, rituals, foods, and dress, we celebrate not only our unique ways of doing things but our commonalities as well. The challenge with such events, however, is to use them in ways that extend beyond the day, to connect them with ideas and understandings that are part of everyday living and that endure in everyone's hearts and minds.

I attended a celebration of Martin Luther King's birthday at the Bronx New School a few years ago that was just that kind of event. It took place in an arts center at a nearby college. Preceded by an international dinner of delicacies from around the world that were brought in by the school's families, as well as by a showing of children's art expressing their understandings of difference that was displayed in the auditorium's foyer, the evening featured a performance from each of the classes in the school.

What I really liked about the performances was that, rather than being a presentation that was only about Martin Luther King, each used King's birthday as an opportunity to connect what they were already studying to broader understandings of difference. For example, a second-grade class, which was in the midst of an extended study about water, presented a play based on the book *Letting Swift River Go*, by Jane Yolen and Barbara Cooney (1995). This is a story of how the reservoir that provides water for the city of Boston was created many years ago by means of literally drowning seven towns. Recounted in the voice of a child whose family had once lived in one of the towns, the story portrays the perspectives of the different people who were affected by the project—the city dwellers who were in need of the water from the reservoir and the different townspeople who had to give up their homes. How differences were handled within these groups, for example, how the graves of the townspeople were dug up and moved to higher ground but not the graves of the Native Americans who had lived in the town long before the other townspeople, is told in a stirring way that leaves all who are presented with it food for thought about how to fairly reconcile the costs of change with the common good. The children made this connection about how events are perceived by different people in different ways and how the impact of an event can vary dramatically, depending on one's status in the community.

Other classes used the occasion of Martin Luther King Day to explore new and expanded perspectives on topics they were in the midst of studying. Ronnie's kindergarten, for example, involved in a study of plants, presented a dance depicting how planting was done in different African cultures. Kendra's fourth-grade class, which at the time was engaged in reading biographies, also created a dance about a book on Bessie Coleman, the first African American woman aviator. Collectively, these performances (the result of collaborations with teaching artist Asma from Dream Yard, an arts organization that sends teaching artists into New York City schools) introduced the children to people, places, cultures, and ideas that connect to but are different from what they had known. What better way to celebrate Martin Luther King's vision for a respectful mosaic than to use the day allotted to his memory as a way of heightening awareness about diverse experiences and perspectives!

As I reflected on the evening on my way home, one thing that stood out for me was how lovingly the teachers interacted with the children during the event. Their pride in the work was contagious, resonating with the children and their families. And the lesson of the evening—seeing the world through others' eyes—made me think about how it must feel as a child to participate in an experience like this. The beauty and magic of the performances, no doubt, offered everyone who experienced them a sense of possibility—about the ability to make beauty, to understand the perspectives of others, to make change, and to make connections with those whose lives, at least on the surface, seem very different and far away. I believe in the power of such experiences to inspire and transform lives. I have no doubt that some of the children who participated that night will carry this sense of possibility with them in their hearts forever.

Infusing Respect for Diversity into Everyday Events

The most profound way to honor differences is to make awareness of and respect for diverse perspectives a part of everyday life. A holiday or special event is not needed for this. It can be infused into any topic or issue.

In Chapter 10, when talking about Ronnie's morning meeting, I described how Ronnie instilled in the children an awareness of others' perspectives—their feelings as well as their viewpoints. To become conscious that the world is seen through different eyes was the point of the comments she directed to the children when she had them engage in voting about the weather or when she called on them to be sensitive to the impact that their words had on each other.

That too was one of the major goals of the Colonial New York study undertaken by Martha's class. Yes, the project ostensibly was designed to help the children learn about the early history of New York City as outlined in the state standards. But of equal importance was Martha's aim to help the children understand and appreciate that different people have different and valid perspectives on a given situation because of their background and life experiences and that, because of people's different circumstances, events affect them differently and lead them to make different choices as they try to resolve life's problems and dilemmas. By assuming different personas during their study, the children got firsthand experience of how one's daily realities influence one's decisions. Additionally, they got to experience firsthand how to acquire the tools to make decisions in the face of varying perspectives. This lesson about diversity is one that all citizens in a democracy need to have. It prepares children for the decisions and challenges they will face as they enter the grown-up world of responsibilities.

CHILDREN LEARN WHAT THEY LIVE

A powerful way to teach children to respect and honor diversity is for them to see adults who do so. When children see teachers giving children what they need, paying attention to what they say, building on their unique strengths and gifts, recognizing differences as positive and welcoming them into the classroom, children develop images for themselves of how to do this with others. They learn what they live. They are keen observers. They turn to adults to make sense of the world. They watch how adults interact with each other and resolve differences. What they see adults do becomes a blueprint for the actions they take in the rest of their lives.

Children Learn What They Live
(Dorothy Law Nolte, 1972)

If children live with criticism, they learn to condemn.
If children live with hostility, they learn to fight.
If children live with ridicule, they learn to feel shy.
If children live with shame, they learn to feel guilty.
If children live with encouragement, they learn confidence.
If children live with tolerance, they learn patience.
If children live with praise, they learn appreciation.
If children live with acceptance, they learn to love.
If children live with approval, they learn to like themselves.
If children live with honesty, they learn truthfulness.
If children live with security, they learn to have faith in
    themselves and those about them.
If children live with friendliness, they learn the world is a
    nice place in which to live.

PART III

Images of Possibility: Schoolwide Structures and Practices

CHAPTER 9

Using Assessment to Support Student Learning

The stories presented in the previous chapters describe a reconceptualization of teaching grounded in understandings of how children learn. In contrast to the transmission-of-knowledge model of teaching that is currently the norm in many schools (based on the notion that learning is the acquisition of known answers to standard problems) (Marshall, 1992), the reconceptualization of teaching presented here is based on the assumption that learning is a process of active construction, emerging from individuals' interactions with experiences and people in meaningful, purposeful contexts. This reconceptualization is integrally connected to a reconceptualization of assessment, as a process that both informs instruction and supports students' learning.

In this chapter I explore issues of assessment, illustrating with examples from the Bronx New School's practices. Throughout the discussion I draw implications about curriculum, instruction, school structures and accountability systems, professional development, home-school relations, and the development of an overall sense of community.

AKEEM'S STORY:
OBSERVING AND DOCUMENTING CHILDREN'S STRENGTHS

I begin with a story of the impact of a teacher's assessment practices on the school life of a child, reconstructed from teachers' observations and reflections. It demonstrates how careful documentation of students calls attention to otherwise hidden strengths that, when used as a resource for teaching, can be of direct benefit to students' growth.

Beginnings

Akeem came to the Bronx New School as a third grader after 3 difficult years in the overcrowded school of his disenfranchised neighborhood. Standardized teaching and testing had already marked him as a failure. He had scored in the lowest percentiles on the standardized reading and math tests administered to all children in the New York City public schools. In addition, his official school cumulative record folder was filled with report cards that consistently brought attention to his troubling behavior. Little information could be found, however, to explain why these judgments had been made.

Right from the start, Akeem stood out in his class because of his frequent outbursts of disruptive behavior. He continually interrupted class and all-school meetings, individual and group lessons, in fact just about any activity in his proximity. At these times a scowl would appear on his otherwise gentle face. He would sneer or mutter sarcastic comments under his breath, hurl projectiles made from rubber bands, erasers, or paper clips across the room, fidget endlessly, or make fun of others in his group.

It didn't take long for school staff to find out that Akeem's disruptive behavior was connected to the fact that he could barely read, write, or do simple math problems. It was whenever he was asked to engage in any activity vaguely related to these things that his disruptions would begin. It seemed that rather than be known for *not* being good at something (in this case it was school-related learning), Akeem preferred to be known for being good at "being bad." Herb Kohl discussed this universal need to be good at *something* in his book *I Won't Learn from You!* (1991).

There were really no provisions in the school system for Akeem's teacher (the Susan described in Chapter 4) to find out about his past. She was only able to do so informally and by accident (at a district staff development session where she met teachers from his prior school). She found out then that Akeem was indeed quite famous, that he was known throughout his old school for an incident in which he had got so angry that he had thrown a chair at his former teacher, and that subsequently he had spent the following term in suspension, out of the classroom, either shadowing a school administrator or sitting idly in the principal's office.

Problem Solving

Susan shared this information about him with her colleagues. Because punishments for his past actions had obviously proved ineffective, and because Bronx New School teachers didn't believe in that kind of punishment anyway, together they searched for other solutions to alleviate Akeem's behavior problems. They came up with an idea: Since they had already determined that Akeem's disruptive behavior bouts were consistently correlated with assignments to do things he could *not* do, the logical way to avoid further disruptive behavior, they hypothesized, was to find things to involve him in that he actually *could* do. This idea seemed to make sense and they all agreed to try it to see if it made a difference. But what were those things Akeem could do? They didn't know. They suspected that he didn't know either.

To discover what it was that Akeem *could* do and what it was that he liked to do, Susan decided to allow him, temporarily, the freedom to choose his own work. He was given his choice of the many rich and varied activities that were available in his classroom. He was also allowed to make his own schedule and was excused from the group meetings that his disruptive behavior had formerly dominated.

Susan observed him closely as he began to try out this new arrangement. He explored the materials in his new classroom, strumming through books, building with math manipulatives and blocks, trying out art materials such as paint and clay and collage materials, "messing about" (Hawkins, 1965) with sand, water, and other science paraphernalia such as batteries, bulbs, wires, and magnets.

Although he initially wandered and tested things out the way a small child does in a room full of toys, Akeem soon began to gravitate to a few types of activities. Dabbling at first, he gradually got deeply involved in building—designing intricate Lego and block constructions as well as sculptures out of junk materials. He meticulously reproduced these constructions in drawings and also spent long periods of time making other drawings from illustrations that he found in books. The more involved he got in this work, the more his disruptive behavior began to subside.

Susan kept track of these developments through regular entries in her journal that documented what he did, how he did it, the issues that arose for him in the course of his work, the areas of his strengths, and those areas in which he needed help.

> During a unit on space he constructs a space shuttle out of a seltzer bottle, cardboard pieces, and other items. He refers to books for help with his work, sits at meetings with the rest of the class now, and is valued by the others for his talents and sought after for advice in these areas.

Based on what she learned from reflecting on this information, Susan adjusted her teaching strategies to his particular needs. She made sure the classroom was amply provisioned with materials for his work—

plenty of found objects, glue, masking tape, paints, clay, old broken superhero figures, scissors, and so on.

Changes

While allowing Akeem to follow his own interests initially created logistical problems for Susan as she balanced his needs with those of the whole class, this was only necessary for a short time. The more involved he got in his chosen work, the less disruptive he became. Soon he began participating in regular class activities. The investment turned out to be well worth the time and energy spent.

Akeem's fidgeting fingers quickly became adept at putting small pieces together, crafting interesting and aesthetic objects and designs. He constructed a set of action figures and wrote a catalog to go with them describing the different figures and what they did. He built a collection of aviation vehicles and wrote an accompanying book that illustrated the history of flight. He made a series of Lego buildings and drawings that were amazingly accurate reproductions of the Empire State Building, the CitiCorp building, and other iconic New York City buildings.

At times his involvement in these projects was so intense that he chose to give up recess to work on them. I'll never forget seeing him one day in the lunchroom, standing near the door, wolfing down his sandwich, hopping from one foot to another, as he impatiently waited for his teacher to pick him up so that he could return to his classroom to finish *writing* (!) his book on the history of flight.

As Akeem became more involved in his newfound work, Susan invited him to share it with the class at end-of-work-time meetings or at the class exhibitions presented at the conclusion of a study. These sessions had formerly been dominated by more academic presentations, such as writing or the outcomes of science experiments. But she soon realized, as a result of her experiences with him, that a classroom limited to only such traditional forms of academic expression excludes different types of children as well as different types of knowledge. She also became aware that the child who is less connected to books and reading and more to other forms of expression such as art feels that when there is no room in school for this kind of activity, there is no room for him or her either. So Susan began to make these materials available in the room every day, to allow children to be active, and to provide a variety of media for their work. Doing this extended the range of what was valued. Everyone was acknowledged as a success in one area or another so that no one felt like a "failure." Not only Akeem, but other children as well, began to understand this inclusive message. They began to feel that there was a place for them in the class.

The more Akeem received recognition for his work, the more his surly look faded. His disruptive episodes all but disappeared. He began to participate in the class schedule of the day, including reading and writing and math workshops. He even cooperated with the reading specialist who began to regularly work with him. It appeared that the validation he had experienced from doing what he was good at had affected his attitude toward his most vulnerable areas. His interests had been strengthened and unleashed by his having the opportunities to pursue them. He began to take risks, try what he couldn't do, ask questions when he didn't understand.

Using Assessment to Inform Teaching

The changes in Akeem that I have described could not have happened if his teacher had not been a careful observer and documenter. Her records of Akeem and his work, collected and reviewed over time, led her to identify not only his weaknesses (all that anyone ever saw before), but also his strengths and his resources. They revealed his exceptional artistic and mechanical abilities—that he was a builder, a doer, a maker of things—as well as his learning style, namely, his interests, tastes, approaches, pace.

Susan put this information to use to serve Akeem better as he struggled with reading and the other "hard stuff" for him. In reading, for example, she saw his overreliance on phonics, inculcated in him by the scripted reading programs used with him by previous teachers, which resulted in his lack of awareness of other strategies that could support him in figuring out the unknown—using the context, focusing on meaning, substituting a word that makes sense, reading on to the end of the sentence, and so on. She noted how his frustration and low self-esteem kept him from taking the risks that are needed to learn new things. She also noted how when he read, his eyes would dwell on the illustrations in a book, and that informed her to allow him plenty of time for soaking up the pictures before attempting the words. This understanding led her to select books for him that contained beautiful, detailed drawings, and it was these kinds of books that he eventually began to eagerly seek out, that engaged him, and that ultimately helped him break into reading independence and fluency. She wrote about this in her records about him:

Today we read two chapters. I read the first page. He went on. He built momentum as he went along. I provided unknown words at first. Then I suggested several strategies: pointing to the words as he goes along (sometimes he needs this but sometimes he doesn't);

going ahead to try the rest of the sentence when he doesn't know the word; using the pictures for clues. I also pointed out different endings of root words such as "er," "ing," and "ed." At the height of his momentum, he was almost reading fluently! Then he slowed down. It seems that he needs to concentrate so hard that he gets exhausted.

Careful observation and documentation of Akeem's work was used not only to analyze and support his learning strategies, it also influenced how Susan shaped the curriculum for the whole class. Tapping into Akeem's passion for building, making, and doing, she included a study of architecture in the class's extended study of their community. As a result, the entire class got involved in trips to famous New York City buildings and bridges, designed their own dream houses, read and wrote about architectural history, and built models of bridges from which they learned about such principles of physics as tension/ compression, load, and sway.

As she did with Akeem, Susan engaged the interests of the other children in the class by providing opportunities to pursue these activities. She provided them with materials and resources that supported them in pursuit of their questions, connected to their past understandings, helped uncover their curiosity and additional questions, and continually stretched their thinking. Along the way she advised and provided lots of opportunities for dialogue and discussion.

In this way Akeem and his classmates integrated new understandings, new ideas, new competencies, and new skills into their prior ones. It was thrilling to watch this all unfold, especially to see Akeem transform and uncover his strengths. He began to actually enjoy school (one teacher observed him skipping his way down the block to school one morning) and to eagerly seek out new opportunities for work. His comment on school, taken from a yearbook at the end of his 5th-grade year was

If you don't know something in another school it's your problem. Here you can work it out. Instead of reading about something, you do it. And because you want to learn about something, you learn more.

SCHOOLWIDE DOCUMENTATION
AND ASSESSMENT OF STUDENT PROGRESS

From its inception, the Bronx New School put into place a schoolwide assessment system. Each element of the system reflects a basic assumption about learning. Based on the belief that learners have a variety of ways of learning and of demonstrating what they know, multiple sources of information are collected over time to give a full picture of children's different strengths and learning styles.

And since it is the school's conviction that the most important purpose of assessment is to inform instruction and support students' learning, many of the assessments are teacher administered as part of the everyday learning life of the classroom. In this way they yield onsite and immediate information that teachers can use to shape further teaching. To be most effective for this purpose, the assessments are designed to reveal not only what students know and can do, but also what strategies students use in the process of learning. Thus, there are few multiple-choice or fill-in-the-blank tests of skills or knowledge, which can yield a correct answer simply from a guess. Rather, most of the assessments used are observations or tasks that involve students in solving real-world problems, performing experiments, writing essays, or doing performances.

Since the school also believes it is important to have close ties with families and the community, opportunities for communication between home and school are built into the assessment system design. And finally, in keeping with the school's emphasis on developing children's capacities for reflection and independent thought, the assessment system includes students in the assessment process—assessing their own learning as well as communicating to others what they have learned.

The school's original assessment system was portfolio based. The portfolios, which traveled with each child from grade to grade and teacher to teacher, housed samples of the children's work, as well as the children's own records (reading lists and written self-assessments) and teacher-kept records (anecdotal notes based on observations and checklists). This information was shared with families at twice-yearly conferences. It also informed the content of written progress reports that were completed and sent home prior to each conference. Another part of the school's early assessment work was faculty involvement in formal group descriptive processes developed by Patricia Carini and the Prospect Center (Carini & Featherstone, 2001). While not all these practices are in place today, they have influenced what is intact and are described in more detail below.

Assessment of Individual Student Work—Portfolios

At the Bronx New School's inception, portfolios were a relatively new assessment practice. Today they are increasingly accepted in classrooms and schools around the nation (Martin-Kniep, 1998; Wiggins,

1989), although their contents and purposes vary from place to place. They range from informal collections of student work, sometimes limited to a single discipline area, to extensive cross-discipline collections of required artifacts that must be completed before promotion from a grade or school (Paulson, Paulson, & Meyer, 1991).

The portfolios developed at the Bronx New School are cumulative and authentic documents of students' progress. They are "cumulative" in that they are gathered over time—they contain evidence of student work from each year of a student's school career. They are "authentic" in that the work within them is produced in natural contexts of the school's everyday learning life. The items of evidence are not specially produced to fulfill a set of predetermined portfolio requirements, but accumulated from the range of activities that naturally occur throughout the course of the school year. The artifacts put into the portfolios are selected by both teachers and students to portray a particular growth issue for a child, to demonstrate a significant development or interest, and to provide an occasional sample of what the student considers to be his or her best effort at a particular point in time. These artifacts are dated to give a sense of the progression of student growth over time. An attempt is made to include representative work of the various studies in which the students have engaged. The goal is to have a range of media from all discipline areas. Samples of children's writing provide evidence of their literacy development as well as their ability to express their growing knowledge in social studies, science, and other content areas. Math journals and samples of math problems demonstrate the strategies children use to solve problems. Drawings and other kinds of artwork as well as photos of three-dimensional projects (models and constructions) document the full range of learning that goes on in classrooms.

Thus, portfolios are meant to give as comprehensive a portrait as possible of students' development over time. They demonstrate students' growth through experiences and difficulties measured in relation to their expectations for themselves as well as in relation to the state's standards of achievement.

Over the years, portfolio documentation helped the Bronx New School develop and maintain continuity in its philosophy, values, and practice. As portfolios travel with children from year to year, throughout the grades, a continuum of information about each child is built. School staff is thus able to collectively come to know individuals well and to share understandings and strategies about how best to support each child's growth. The cohesiveness provided by this approach is appropriately described by the ancient African proverb "It takes a whole village to raise a child."

At my last visit to the Bronx New School, portfolios were still in use. While some of the instruments used to collect information about the children (including some forms mandated by New York City's Department of Education) have been updated, the purposes for assessment remain the same as in the early years of the school. In an interview, Martha explained to me how she uses portfolios as a means of reflecting on her students' growth:

> We save the kids' work. They periodically go through it and pick out what they want to save. It's actually really neat when they get to 5th grade because we have a file that follows them from class to class. It has their K work . . . a few pieces of work from each grade. I ask kids to pick out pieces that show their best work and also pieces that show their learning. For some of those we're picking out pieces of work where they're going to be making revisions, because they've learned something and they want to change it. So one of the things we need to do is look through our social studies notebooks and pick out the pages we want to photocopy and put in the portfolio.

Teacher-Kept Records

Teacher-kept records of children are an important part of a schoolwide assessment system. These can include anecdotal records based on observations of students, inventories or checklists of skill development, and notes from conferences and meetings held with students about various areas of their work. Filled with detailed descriptions and examples of children's learning styles and interests, the strategies they use effectively as well as those that are in need of support in reading, writing, and math, dated teacher records can be used to keep track of the progress of individual children.

Class records can also document the developing knowledge of a group as a whole. These can be kept on large chart paper that can be taped to classroom walls. Charts such as the one shown in Figure 9.1 can be used to note children's prior knowledge and understandings about a topic, children's questions about it, their observations from activities or experiments in relation to it, their answers and comments in response to the original questions, and their new questions arising from their study. These records can be referred to repeatedly in the course of a study, chronicling the journey of the class' investigations and guiding what is to come next.

FIGURE 9.1. Clap chart

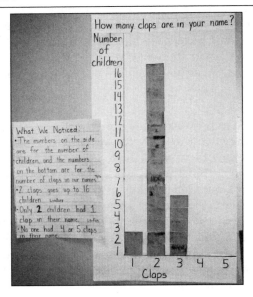

Teachers each have their own ways of keeping track of their students' learning. Some jot down observations on note cards that they carry around with them or on "stickies" that they paste into a notebook at the end of the day. Still others do this in a notebook with dividers that have sections allocated for each child. Some teachers enter quick notes in these during the day; others wait to write longer reflections during preparation periods, lunch, or after-school hours.

In the early years of the Bronx New School, teachers pioneered literacy assessments that have since become accepted into the mainstream. Everyone learned how to do running records (Clay, 2007), a systematic way to document students' reading that helps teachers become aware of exactly what children are doing and what strategies they are using in the course of learning to read. In a running record a teacher notes the number and type of errors made by a student, the number of words read incorrectly but substituted with meaningful alternatives, the number of words that the student omitted, the number of times the student was able to correct him- or herself, as well as the number of times the student needed teacher assistance. This kind of record is particularly helpful for understanding and assisting a child who is a beginning reader.

To put all this assessment information into context, developmental continuums—descriptions of significant behaviors that can be observed as children move through stages from emergent to experienced literacy—were created in the early years of the Bronx New School. Informed by assessments that were first being created when the school was new, such as the Primary Language Record (Barrs, Ellis, Hester, & Thomas, 1990) and the Work Sampling System (Meisels, Jablon, Marsden, Dichtelmiller, Dorfman, & Steele, 1995), these continuums provide a comprehensive picture of how a student is able to manage text while also revealing specific areas of literacy development the student is or is not mastering. Today this approach to looking at student progress has been incorporated into other assessments that are used around the country as well as in New York State assessments (Falk, Ort, & Moirs, 2007).

Student-Kept Records

Children at the Bronx New School have always been involved in assessing their progress. In the past and today, they kept and keep records of their projects, their reading and writing, and their reflections on their learning. In reading logs, journals, or forms made by the teachers, they document what they read, when they read it, and their thoughts about what they have read. This method of keeping track is particularly helpful in classes that use a wide range of texts rather than a single basal reader or textbook. The children's documentation of what they read independently at school as well as at home serves as a record of continuity and accountability to both the child and the teacher.

Student-kept records are also used in other subjects. Math journals document how children's abilities progress in computation and problem solving. Social studies notebooks keep track of the knowledge gained through the different studies the class has engaged in. (These came in quite handy for the children in Martha's class, as described in an earlier chapter, when the class, during their study of Colonial New York, consulted their journals to locate facts they had learned in an earlier study of the Constitution.)

Progress Reports

Traditional grades have never been a part of assessment at the Bronx New School. Instead, progress reports offer a summary of students' growth in many aspects of their learning. Currently in use is a progress report mandated by the New York City Department of Education, which evaluates students' work in different areas on a scale of 1–4. Most teachers, however, supplement that report with their own and their students' reflections. Each report is followed by a conference (discussed below) between the teacher, the child, and his or her family.

The reflective part of the progress report was first developed in the early years of the school. Culled from the detailed observations and documentation of students' work that teachers keep over time, it focuses on children's strengths, framing areas that need to be strengthened as "vulnerabilities" to be worked on, rather than as deficits to remediate. The goal is to give a detailed portrait of the child, framed in the perspective of the continuum of growth, and presented through the light of support, not criticism.

Descriptive, rather than evaluative, language is an important feature of this kind of assessment. In contrast to evaluative language, which often judges the learner based on the product of his or her work, descriptive language focuses on *how* something happens, noting the process as well as the product. It holds the judgment of the observer in abeyance, focusing instead on unpacking the details of what the learner does and how he or she does it. The descriptions below illustrate the difference. Compare these statements about Steven's progress found in a draft narrative report completed by his teacher shortly after she joined the school community with the same teacher's later version, completed after learning more about how to observe and record children at work in the classroom (from Falk, 1994, p. 6):

Early observation	*Later observation*
Steven has an excellent vocabulary.	Steven uses a rich variety of descriptive words in his writing.
Steven does outstanding work.	Steven works independently and intensely. He thinks critically, takes risks in putting forward new ideas, and is thorough in attention to details of presentation.
Steven has excellent math skills.	Steven is fluid in his thinking about number concepts. He can generally find several solutions to a problem and is able to explain them to others in a clear way.

In contrast to the earlier evaluative example, the feedback containing more description explains what makes Steven's vocabulary and math skills "excellent," what about his work warrants the characterization of "outstanding." It provides Steven's teachers, his parents, and himself with a better understanding of *how* he does what he does.

As descriptions in this vein accumulate, they paint a rich picture of each student as a learner. This picture helps students, their families, and other teachers to recognize students' strengths so that they can be built on further. The picture also helps to identify areas of students' work that are in need of support so that plans can be made for how to address them. Karen, a reading support teacher at the school, explained how this approach to assessment enabled her to be more responsive to her student Roberto and to communicate more effectively with his family:

> The documentation that I kept of my work with Roberto showed the ways he grew as a reader that were not evident from his scores on the reading tests. The reading records I had regularly kept on him . . . documented how he was recognizing more words, how his miscues [mistakes, errors] were becoming increasingly related to the meaning of the text, how he was correcting himself more frequently, and how he was reading longer, more complicated passages. This reassured me, as well as Roberto and his family, about his progress and gave me concrete suggestions for how they could support his reading at home. (Falk, 1994, p. 7)

Parents' Responses

Parents really appreciate getting the kind of detailed information about their children's progress that is revealed through teachers' descriptive documentation. Although they *do* want to know how their child is doing in relation to the rest of the world—"This is a third-grade reading level" or "This child is on par with other first graders"—parents also really want to know details about their child as a learner. The more they know about the strategies their child is mastering, the approaches that characterize the child, the books the child is reading, and the behaviors the child is exhibiting, the more able they are to understand and assist their child's learning at home. Written comments such as the one below from parents in response to their children's reports testify to this fact:

> The developmental information in the reports is absolutely essential in order for me to better understand my child's developmental stage. I appreciate the lengthy comments provided by the teachers.

Family Conferences

In addition to progress reports, family conferences—a meeting between the teacher and the significant people in the student's life (including the student)—are another vehicle to share information about the development of children's learning. At the Bronx New School, these are scheduled events, lasting anywhere from 15 to 30 minutes (sometimes longer if needed) to discuss the progress of the child as well as any questions or concerns that family members may have. The child's work is on hand so that families can have firsthand contact with the concrete evidence of the child's learning.

When children are included in the conference about them, they are invited to reflect on their growth and also to voice their concerns and impressions about life in school. This enables the adults in a child's life to learn how he or she thinks and to see how much the child has grown. In some classes, the children not only participate in the conference, they actually lead it. They prepare a presentation of their work in the different curriculum areas. With their portfolios displayed, the children point out to their families what they have done, what they are still working on, how they have grown, what they consider to be their best work, what areas they want to get better at, and what they want to work on next. Some teachers even have children write their own progress reports or write responses to the reports their teachers have written. These practices give the children the sense that they can be authorities in their own learning. As I overheard one teacher instruct her class as they prepared for an upcoming family conference, "You are the ones who know yourselves best."

The conference is designed to take children seriously, engaging in conversations with them and listening to their ideas. These important interactions, too often left out of children's lives, help children understand themselves. After all, we come to know who we are through the feedback we receive from others. As the philosopher Cicero once said: "If I had not my circle of listeners, I would not have the power to speak."

Another purpose of the family conference, besides sharing information with the family about the child's work inside the school, is to obtain information from the family about the child and the child's life outside school. Families are encouraged to share knowledge about their children's interests, dispositions, and contexts for learning. They are also encouraged to ask questions and to participate in providing direction and plans for future work. This aspect of the family conference is a demonstration of the value the school places on the family as a critical resource for the child's growth and learning.

All in all, family conferences build a sense of community in the school. Including children and families, inviting them to be contributors as well as receivers of knowledge, builds trust in the school and benefits all who are involved.

ISSUES FOR TEACHERS

Documenting student work, using it to inform instruction, and communicating information to children and families raises challenges for teachers. Some of the challenges that teachers who engage in this kind of work have grappled with are learning how to observe children and adopt a descriptive rather than evaluative stance; using assessment information to shape teaching so that it is responsive to children's understandings, questions, and interests; and figuring out how to balance teaching that is responsive to children with the demands of preparing for high-stakes tests.

Learning How to Observe

To do the kind of assessment that has been described here, teachers need to learn how to observe and document what children do. They need to learn *what* to observe and *how* to document it in a descriptive manner. This involves learning how to see and note details as well as how to put judgment and personal feelings aside. The earlier example of Steven's teacher's struggle to move away from evaluative language in her report of his work epitomizes this challenge.

When teachers at the Bronx New School first began to document the work of their students in these ways, many felt overwhelmed by what seemed the enormity of the task. They complained that detailed record keeping took too much time and that it would be much easier and less time-consuming to keep track of students' progress in their heads. However, through their experiences of writing down their observations—from a variety of settings in a variety of ways—most recognized that they were learning more about their students from the observing/documenting process than they had ever imagined they could. They began to realize that observing and recording what children did was enabling them to see things they had not noticed before.

As they got accustomed to collecting evidence and keeping written records, they realized that memory of the details and the nuance that makes each child visible does indeed escape them in the blur of time passed; it is the details in the evidence collected about a child that gives them perspective on what is really going on. Jotting down and reflecting thus became part of their "teacherly" ways of life. In much the same way that a researcher gathers evidence to better understand the question he or she is studying, teachers, too, assumed the researcher stance. The children became the subjects of their research and they adopted an evidence-based approach to the teaching/learning process that informed the instructional decisions they made.

Adjusting Teaching to Be Responsive to Children's Understandings, Questions, and Interests

Teachers who become adept at observing are subsequently challenged to learn how to use these observations to inform their teaching and shape curriculum. After they find out what children know and understand, they need to learn how to gear activities and experiences to deepen children's understandings, clarify their misconceptions, and respond to their questions. They need to do this in ways that build on children's interests and use their strengths as resources. This involves moving away from a "teacher as dispenser of knowledge" approach to a "teacher as facilitator" approach. It also means that teachers have to broaden their view of abilities.

When Howard Gardner first enumerated his theory of multiple intelligences, he wrote: "Only if we expand and reformulate our view of what counts as human intellect will we be able to devise more effective ways of educating it" (1983, p. 4).

Some of the ways that the Bronx New School has tried to devise "more effective ways of educating" have been described in earlier chapters. These include provisioning classrooms with a wide range of materials and organizing the rooms for active learning, providing ample opportunities for group collaboration, grouping classes and groups within classes heterogeneously, and offering experiences that allow for multiple entry points to learning for children with differing strengths and intelligences. Teachers thus move away from standardized approaches that require everyone to do the same thing in the same way. As they come to understand that no uniform teaching strategy or curriculum recipe is equally effective for all students, they move toward a differentiated instruction—one that provides different kinds of learners with different pathways to achieve mastery of important common concepts and skills (Tomlinson, 2004). John Dewey described this kind of teaching many years ago:

> To imposition from above is opposed expression and cultivation of individuality; to external discipline is opposed free activity; to learning from texts and teachers, learning through experience; to acquisition of isolated skills and techniques by drill, is opposed acquisition of them as means of attaining ends which make direct vital appeal; to preparation for a more or less remote future is opposed making the most of the opportunities of present life; to static aims and materials is opposed acquaintance with a changing world. (1938, pp. 19–20)

Unfortunately, teaching that looks like Dewey's description is still rare. Highly skilled educators are needed to do it, and these we still do not have enough of as a result of our society's general lack of investment in education. But another impediment to this kind of teaching is the testing that currently dominates schooling.

Balancing Good Teaching and Testing Pressures

Casting a pall over teaching and assessment practices that are responsive to how children learn are the pressures that come from the testing and accountability policies of our cities, states, and federal government. As the years have gone by since the Bronx New School was established, these pressures have increased. Test scores are published in the newspapers, ranking schools based on how well their students perform. More recently, in addition to this, schools are issued report cards, and principals (and in some places, teachers) are rated and rewarded with bonuses based on the scores their students receive. Children too are awarded money and other gifts for the scores they attain on tests. Likewise, they are often punished for low scores by being held over in their grade. Despite vocal opposition to these policies and all that has been written about their harmful effects (Darling-Hammond, 1991, 2006, 2007; Jones & Egley, 2004; McNeil, 2000; Nichols, Glass, & Berliner, 2005), testing continues to be the voice that speaks loudest about a school's effectiveness. This state of affairs creates great tensions for teachers and administrators. We are torn between two responsibilities— teaching the way children learn (in developmentally appropriate and culturally responsive ways that challenge a wide range of learners to think critically, to problem solve, and to apply knowledge to real-world problems) versus adequately preparing children to do well on tests that generally emphasize recall of facts and skills in one-dimensional (paper-and-pencil rather than performance-based) ways.

This tension creates great anxiety for school people, especially those most committed to teaching the way children learn. Many teachers have spoken out about this issue. In conversations I have had with many, they share how painful it is to subject children to the tests; how frustrated they are that the progress their students have made throughout the year often doesn't show up on the tests; how despite the fact that the tests are only a snapshot from one moment in time, the decisions made based on them can profoundly affect children's futures.

Despite their concerns about the limitations of tests, educators at the Bronx New School have always been mindful of the seriousness of the consequences the tests hold for their students. As a result, the school has always made an effort to prepare students to do well on them. All agree, however, that the best test preparation is to have children experience a rich curriculum. Within the context of meaningful and purposeful classroom activities, teachers consciously and explicitly weave the skills and knowledge of the standards. This is done with a commitment to *never* allow testing to drive the curriculum.

In addition to providing children with a rich curriculum interlaced with careful attention to skills, another strategy to help children do well on tests is to help them understand how test formats work and to give them practice in test-taking skills. This kind of test preparation needs to begin by differentiating it from "real" learning activities. It should be introduced several weeks prior to the official test, when teachers expose children to the format of the tests, teaching them how to use the separate answer sheets that come with the test booklets as well as how to fill in the bubbles of the multiple-choice questions. It also needs to include teaching children strategies for how to narrow down the options of the multiple-choice answers and how to avoid the "tricks" of the test.

In my years after leaving the Bronx New School, I devoted a good chunk of time to working on assessment/accountability issues—trying to help ease the tensions between good teaching and assessment. I worked with a group of educators who urgently felt the need for better assessments that capture a fuller range of information about what students know and can do, while respecting the need for the public to have understandable and clear ways of holding schools accountable. We worked on developing a design for a standards-based performance assessment system for our state's education department. Together teachers from across the state invented prototypes of performance assessments and portfolios that could capture a fuller picture of students' learning than the multiple-choice and fill-in-the-blank tests that previously had dominated standardized testing.

Although the authentic performance tasks and collections of student work we created were enthusiastically embraced by many teachers and were judged by many experts to meet professional standards for reliability and validity, we had difficulty convincing policy makers that we had found a better way. Our innovations were never fully institutionalized. While some aspects of our work were incorporated into the current state-assessment system, moving it toward a more performance-oriented evaluation, the high-stakes policies connected to assessment results remained largely unaffected. As the years have gone by, in fact, the innovations that made their way into the assessment system were overshadowed by the policies surrounding them, which have actually become even more high stakes.

So, sadly, assessment and accountability continue to have serious problems that are harmful to many children, teachers, administrators, and schools. We educators still face enormous challenges in this regard. To address these challenges we need to educate ourselves and the public about the aspects of testing that are not good for children and continue our efforts to put into place assessments and assessment policies that offer useful information and that support good teaching and learning.

CHAPTER 10

Involving Families in School Life

Parents and other family members are a child's first teachers. All policies regarding families in a school need to be guided by this fact. We educators must not forget that families have important understandings about their children that need to be valued; that children come to school with a wealth of knowledge from their backgrounds and cultures; and that, since learning builds on prior knowledge and experience, we need to know about and be respectful of all aspects of the backgrounds that children bring with them to school.

The research is clear that children's development is maximized when they experience the support of caring adults in families, schools, and communities (Brown & Reeve, 1987; Rogoff, 2003; Sampson, Sharkey, & Raudenbush, 2007). Not only does the social and economic environment in which children grow up (prenatally and into the early years of life) affect the quality and extent of their learning; the quality of their relationships, especially the primary caregiving relationship, has a powerful impact on how they develop and what they learn (Bowman, Donovan, & Burn, 2001). Close and dependable early relationships that provide love, nurturance, and security, that are responsive to needs, foster connections, and encourage engagement and exploration, are what promote optimal development. When children do not have such a nurturing environment—or at least one close and dependable relationship—their development can be seriously disrupted (Garbarino, Dubrow, Kostelny, & Pardo, 1998).

Putting this knowledge into effect in schools means involving families as partners in the learning community and engaging them in various ways to play an important role in supporting their children's learning. Besides making the school accessible to families, opportunities also need to be provided to enhance their understandings of the educational philosophy and practices of the school, especially when these differ from the ways that family members have been educated in the past. The more family members understand and support what goes on in school, the more they will be able to assist their children's learning.

Founded by a joint effort between families and educators, the Bronx New School has been successful at maintaining active family involvement over the years. In this chapter I describe communication and governance structures developed throughout the school's history that have been effective at nurturing home-school partnerships. Although family involvement has been intrinsic to the Bronx New School's culture because of the prominent role that families played in its creation, I share images of what has been done over the years in the hopes that some of the ideas can be applicable to other school communities.

COMMUNICATION VEHICLES BUILD COMMUNITY

More than anything else I can think of, lots of avenues for communication between home and school help to build common goals and understandings between families and teachers and thus a more effective and cohesive educational community. Communication avenues need to exist at both the classroom and the school level. At the classroom level these can include teacher curriculum letters, questionnaires, phone calls to family members, homework notes, progress reports, family conferences, and class meetings. At the school level, communication can be facilitated through newsletters from the director/principal or the parents association and all-school meetings with families.

Teacher Curriculum Letters and Homework Notes

At the Bronx New School teachers regularly send home a "curriculum letter" (on a weekly, biweekly, or monthly basis), which contains written explanations of the studies and activities taking place in their classrooms. These classroom newsletters offer highlights of recent learning experiences, explain different educational practices (for example, what the "morning meeting" time of the day is and how it promotes literacy skills), and make suggestions to caregivers about how to support children's academic learning (for example, helpful hints for reading aloud to children, for how to choose appropriate books, for how to introduce a new book, and for how to listen to children read). To give a sense of what I mean, Figure 10.1 shows an excerpt from Ronnie's curriculum letter.

Sometimes teachers also use their curriculum letters to share resources they think might be of interest to families, such as helpful parenting tips or an inspirational poem. They can ask parents to fill out questionnaires that provide information to enhance the teachers' knowledge of each child. Here is an example of such a questionnaire sent out to kindergarten families toward the beginning of the school year:

FIGURE 10.1. Ronnie's curriculum letter

Supporting Reading at Home

Dear Parent:

Good readers:

- have a group of known words that they can read and write without help;
- use the pictures and what they know about story language and letter sounds while reading;
- catch most of their own mistakes by listening and thinking about the story while reading;
- are able to try different things when they're stuck on a word, such as looking at pictures, thinking about the story, rereading from the beginning of the sentence, and looking for what is known about the problem word;
- fix most of their mistakes without help;
- keep discovering new things about print.

The activities you will receive promote good reading habits.

Sincerely,

Ronnie

Family questionnaire

- How does your child feel about coming to kindergarten? How do you feel? Do you have any special concerns?
- Has your child been to other schools before? Where? For how long? How was the experience?
- Are there other children in the family? How do they get along?
- What kinds of things does your child like best to do? Active or quiet?
- Does your child like books yet? Is he or she read to? How often? What are his or her favorites?

- How is your child's appetite? Any food allergies? Food aversions? Are there school snacks we should avoid? Any health problems?

Sometimes teachers ask families to participate in events or contribute needed items for the class. Here is a letter sent to solicit family involvement in classroom life:

Dear Parents,

There are many opportunities for parents to become involved in our classroom life. Let us know how you might like to participate. Please check all that apply and include any particulars:

__ I can participate on class trips. (Mon., Tues., Wed., etc.)
__ I can help with sewing.
__ I would like to volunteer in the classroom to help with cooking and other special projects.
__ I know how to use a computer and can help with "publishing" children's work.
__ I would like to share my job or talent with the class.

Teachers communicate in other ways, too. Some send letters with the homework, explaining the homework's purpose, the skills embedded in it, as well as instructions for how caregivers can help their children with their assignments. Because teaching methods now are so different from what they were when most caregivers were in school, suggestions for how to support children with their homework can often make a critical difference in their learning. These help, for example, to prevent children from getting confused because they receive one message ("carry the one") about how to do subtraction when the school is teaching a different way (that the 1 in the 10s column really represents a 10). Figure 10.2 shows another example of a letter from Ronnie's class that explains what the homework is all about.

To facilitate the flow of communication between home and school, most classrooms set up some kind of a system to ensure that the curriculum letters, homework letters, and other important school messages are gathered in one place and actually get home. Martha, like other Bronx New School teachers, has a "take-home folder" for each child. She requires that caregivers sign a return slip, usually attached to the letter, to indicate that the message has been read.

FIGURE 10.2. Ronnie's homework letter

Morning News Homework Starts Today

The Morning News is a shared writing activity. The children give suggestions and help compose the sentences for the class news. We decide together what to write first, last, etc. As I write each sentence on a chart, the children help identify some of the beginning letters in the words and help spell some of the words. After the news is finished, we read it together. Then we play the "detective game." The children put on their detective hats before starting the game.

In this game, the children are asked to search for particular words, letters, spellings, etc. For example, detectives are asked to search for the word *October*. Children who can locate the word *October* raise their hands. One child is picked to come up to the chart and find the word. S/he circles the word with a marker. Sometimes the children are asked to find two words that are exactly the same. If they can locate two identical words, they circle both words using the same color marker. Suggestions for playing the game are attached to today's news homework.

Please remember:

- Your child needs different color markers or crayons to play the game.
- We want children to learn the difference between letters and words, so we treat them differently. *Words are circled* and *letters and parts of words are highlighted.*
- We use a different color crayon or marker to circle each pair of matching words—words that look exactly alike.

Class Meetings

Meetings between a class teacher and his or her students' family members are a useful way for members of the classroom community to get acquainted with each other and to have an opportunity to address their questions and concerns. Most schools hold such gatherings at least once during the year. Teachers at the Bronx New School do so also. At these meetings they often engage family members in the same activities that the children do during the day to give a feel for what the children's school experience is like. In the early childhood classrooms, for example, caregivers who attend such meetings get a chance to build with blocks, work with math manipulatives, and use other materials that the children have in class, as well as participate in a class meeting. "Hands-on" experiences like these bring understandings about learning to life more deeply than just talking about them can.

Notes from the School Leader

When I was the director of the Bronx New School, each week I wrote a newsletter for families and other members of the school community. Besides informing readers about day-to-day happenings that were taking place in the school, the newsletter regularly contained articles that explained the implications or underlying purposes of the school's educational practices. In it, I explained my views on such topics as literacy development, new standards for mathematics, and the problems of standardized tests. Often I would also include articles about an educational issue from a magazine or journal, other educational resources, or suggestions for parents (lists of good multicultural books, for example). In addition to explaining the school's teaching practices, I would write about issues pertaining to child development and parenting concerns, such as discipline, the stress children experience leading up to holiday time, concerns about excessive television watching or video game use, how to handle children's questions about sensitive subjects, or how to communicate with children in constructive ways. Other subsequent heads of the school have done similar things. Here is an example of a letter about discipline that I sent home to school family members one year:

Children and Discipline

So often, when adults relate to children, we fall back on the methods that were used with us when we were small—spanking, yelling, name-calling, punishments. They come so naturally that we don't even think about them. But there are other ways to discipline children that can help them to develop their own inner controls so that we adults don't have to be their constant police officers. These are ways to help children to develop a good feeling about themselves and to develop their ability to care about other people.

This kind of disciplining is a way of guiding behavior rather than of controlling behavior. It is a learning/teaching process. Its goal is to develop inner controls in the child.

Some suggestions for how to do this are

1. Listen to your child, empathize with his/her feelings, but forge ahead with what must be done. "I know it is hard to wait, but everyone needs to have a turn."

2. State what needs to be done in positive terms. Use the word "do" more often than "don't." For example. "Put the blocks on the shelf when you're done" rather than "Don't leave blocks all over."

3. Speak to your child's behavior, not to his/her overall character. This applies to positive as well as negative actions. Say "I cannot let you hit her. It will hurt her." rather than "You naughty girl, why are you always hitting?" or "That was very helpful of you to clean up your room." rather than "You are such a good girl!"

4. Say what you mean directly. "Settle down now. It's eight o'clock." is very vague. Rather, say, "It's time for bed. Let's read a book."

5. Give children choices whenever you can. When children are very young, give only two acceptable (to you) choices. As they get older, negotiate what are acceptable choices. Don't say, "Shall we go to bed now?" if you mean "It's bedtime now." Instead, add, "It's bedtime now. Would you like to read a book or listen to a record?"

6. When you must make decisions for children, explain your reasons whenever possible, rather than saying, "Because I said so." Try instead: "You have to wash your hands because you've been playing outside and they are dirty."

7. Redirect unacceptable behavior. When you see your child hitting or biting in anger, stop him/her and say, "I can see that you are very angry. You need to tell David how you feel with words and not with hitting."

8. Use distraction techniques—joke around, motivate toward the next activity to be done. For example, talk about how nice it will be to play outside once we get dressed. Or, try an alternate choice or activity—"I see you don't want the apple; how about an orange?"; "I can't let you kick him when you are angry, but we can go outside and kick this ball."

9. State your frustrations. Instead of venting frustration by yelling, hitting, or name-calling, state your feelings nonabusively: "When you act like this, it makes me feel very angry. You need to cooperate now. Please put this book on the shelf."

Helping children to grow into independent beings who have inner controls and feelings of self-worth is no easy task. It is difficult for us adults to keep our cool and maintain a positive attitude of respect for children when they frequently do outrageous things! But remember—growth and development involve testing adult controls. Even a misbehaving child might be showing creativity, consistency, perseverance, or even courage. Focus on your child's strengths. Notice even small improvements. Give lots of encouragement for your child's efforts.

Your child is deserving of your respect, courtesy, and nonjudgmental guidance. When children are treated in this way, we earn their trust and they feel our acceptance and love.

All-School Family Meetings

All-school family meetings are a vehicle for discussion about issues in the school or education in general. They offer an opportunity for the school community to explore topics of interest such as literacy development, math, testing, conflict resolution, communication and discipline skills, sibling rivalry, health education, or issues related to cultural diversity. Whether led by outside "experts" or representatives of the school staff, meetings about educational issues can serve as forums for ongoing discussion of the school's philosophy, values, and practice. Regular conversation about the important ideas that give a school its identity ensures that the ideas stay up to date and endure.

To ensure maximum attendance at parent meetings, the Bronx New School holds them in the evenings to accommodate parents and caregivers who work during the day. While this meeting time is good for those families who work, it presents other challenges such as child care and transportation. These challenges were addressed in several ways when the school was first set up. For those families for whom it was a hardship to pay for the additional round-trip transportation that an evening meeting would require, a transportation fund was set up. Those who were in need could get reimbursed for their bus, subway, or car fare. Likewise, for families who had no one to stay with their children, child care was provided at every meeting. And because the children were present, the meetings were held early so that everyone could get home at a reasonable hour. To make it easier for everyone to get to the school at an early hour, meetings were often preceded by a potluck supper, with the school providing beverages and dessert. Attention to these issues resulted in a large percentage of families participating in school meetings.

These multiple forums for communication enable families and educators to exchange ideas, express their questions and concerns, and come to understand each other's perspectives. Doing this is critical to developing the family support that is essential for a school's philosophy and practices to endure. The story that follows is an example of how this support can be won.

The Power of Multiple Avenues of Communication

Worry about reading occupies the energies of many families who have young children. Because the consequences of problems in this area can be literally life threatening for some students, especially in this era of high-stakes testing, reading is understandably a highly charged concern. As in many schools where literacy development is approached in a holistic, contextualized manner, families at the Bronx New School are often worried about how and when their children will become independent and fluent readers. Because the school's literacy program focuses on learning skills in meaningful contexts rather than through isolated drills on skills (a different method from what many caregivers experienced themselves when they attended school), when their child's progress lags or is not readily apparent, families often succumb to a desire for the known and the familiar (even when memories of that are unpleasant) and crave a return to more traditional methods. A high-intensity time for concerns about reading often occurs in the first-grade year.

Despite current pressures on children to learn to read at ever earlier ages, experienced teachers and child development experts know that it is not uncommon for some children to become independent, fluent readers as late as the third grade (Bussis, Chittenden, Amarel, & Klausner, 1985). But family concerns and worries (fed by a school system driven by tests and test scores rather than developmental principles) often overflows well before this time. The experience of Monica, a Bronx New School first grader, and her mother demonstrates how these concerns can be addressed.

Monica's mother was filled with anxieties about what seemed to be Monica's slow progress in reading. She could not help but compare her daughter with other children she met in the playground or at parties who seemed more advanced. Monica's mother brought these concerns to her child's teacher, the school's reading specialist, the school psychologist, and the school's director. She also raised her concerns at class meetings, whole-school meetings, and PTA meetings. Each time she was responded to with information about literacy development in general as well as with detailed information about her own child's progress. Teachers tried to assure her that Monica possessed many strengths and that, in addition, she was making steady gains in reading. Their lengthy progress reports, based on their observational records and the collected samples of Monica's work, which they shared at numerous family conferences and conversations, helped Monica's mother see Monica's strategies for learning and what the teachers were doing to support her.

Sensing that Monica's mother's concerns were shared by other families in the school who were too reticent to speak up, the teachers and I set up a series of meetings for families about literacy development. These meetings featured speakers as well as videos that offered depictions of how different children made their ways into reading. Additionally, we wrote numerous articles for the school community explaining different aspects of literacy development. We also circulated reprints from educational journals for those who were interested in more information.

These efforts, combined with the fact that within a few months Monica began to read independently (to visibly exhibit the learning we knew she had been internally constructing all along), calmed Monica's mother's anxieties. She reflected on her feelings at the end of the year in a letter she wrote to the school's parents association newsletter:

> It wasn't until Monica became an independent reader that I came to appreciate and understand what the school's philosophy really meant—that each student has a particular way of learning. I couldn't relax enough while Monica was still struggling to appreciate what the process really entailed. I was too anxious, never having experienced this before. I didn't trust that all along Monica was learning and putting the pieces together. But now I have experienced that the way of teaching here really works and I understand much more about teaching and learning. I plan to share my understandings with parents of younger children to help ease them through the process of change. I feel like I need to publicly thank and apologize to the school staff for all the doubts and questions that I raised. (Falk, 1994, p. 29)

Monica's mother owed no apology for her anxieties. It is the job of parents to advocate for what they think is best for their children, to keep asking questions and raising concerns until they feel satisfied that they are addressed. The school's job, in response, should be to provide families with information about child development, about learning, and about how it all applies to the particularities of each child. As families and educators work through this process, educators (hopefully) heighten their sensitivity to family concerns. Families, in turn, hopefully, arrive at deeper understandings and greater trust in their school and the learning process itself.

STRUCTURES TO SUPPORT FAMILY INVOLVEMENT

Other school structures also contribute to enhanced involvement and understandings between home and school.

Parent Coordinator

One such structure is the position of parent coordinator, created many years ago at the Bronx New School and funded by a foundation grant before it became an institutionalized position in the New York City school system. The parent coordinator is responsible for facilitating smooth communication between home and school, for helping the different parts of the community—staff, parents, and parent organizations—to work together efficiently, for creating liaisons between the school and community resources, and for serving as an advocate and resource for families within the school itself as well as in the larger school system.

The parent coordinator at the Bronx New School is a resource for families. She does things like putting together a directory of all families in the school so that everyone can easily contact each other, bringing educational workshops to the school (such as the diversity events discussed in Chapter 8), and arranging for leadership training workshops and educational workshops for families to attend in the larger community. The parent coordinator also seeks out resources for children—summer camps, after-school tutoring programs, and educational programs at the public library, local colleges, or community institutions. She also notifies families of important community meetings, distributes literature about educational issues, and brings resources (such as free book programs) into the school.

Parents Association Activities

Working in conjunction with the parent coordinator, a parents association committed to reaching out to and involving all families organizes many different kinds of activities. Over the years at the Bronx New School, Halloween parties, Mother's Day breakfasts, and concerts and other cultural performances have offered families an opportunity to socialize together with their children in fun and educational contexts.

Parents have found ways to participate in and contribute to the school in other ways as well. One parent, a nurse, presented first-aid workshops for the staff. Another, a graphic designer, created a logo and T-shirts for the school. A workshop on newspaper writing was given to the children in some of the older classes by a parent who is a journalist. A father who is an amateur juggler performed at a meeting of the whole school. A carpenter made frames for a school paper-making project. Other parents have made other contributions: one brought a dancer friend to conduct workshops with the different classes; another's brother, a professional singer, gave a concert for the school community; another arranged a lecture/demonstration on African dance.

Other parents have donated supplies. One holiday time, the teachers got together to write a letter to families requesting that instead of purchasing a gift for their teacher, they make a contribution to their child's class or to the school as a whole. The staff made a wish list of items that ranged in cost from only a few dollars to more expensive items. Among these were markers, games, scissors, puzzles, playing cards, photography books, atlases, children's almanacs, dictionaries, thesauri, the *Guinness Book of World Records*, class subscriptions to children' magazines, photo albums, CDs/DVDs, tapes, clay, glue, paint, globes, balls, jump ropes, pet food, photocopy paper, and disposable cameras. Families were given the option of purchasing an item themselves or making a financial contribution toward a purchase. The idea was to enable everyone to enjoy the holiday spirit together in a lasting way.

Parents Association Newsletter

A parents association newsletter can give voice to parents' concerns and serve as a communication vehicle between families and educators. In the early years of the Bronx New School, the parents association published a newsletter three or four times during the school year. Each issue contained announcements about interesting events (a Latin American book fair, Family Day at el Museo del Barrio, school board elections); news about community members' lives; information about useful services or resources; articles about parenting or education; or questionnaires developed by the parents association asking for feedback on events, the curriculum, fund-raising activities, or suggestions for how people might want to get more involved. Feedback from families has been a crucial barometer to guide future activities and actions. Below are some comments given anonymously in response to a questionnaire that was sent out by the parents association at the conclusion of the school's first year. These confirmed that we were moving toward the realization of the goals that had led to the founding of the school:

In our old school my child felt pressure, fear, stress, and expectation that all had to do the same thing. The BNS (Bronx New School) has been accepting of her gifts.

The BNS is fostering my K child's sense of independence as a learner and thinker.

In our old school, parental involvement was actively discouraged; here it is encouraged.

I like the integrated educational techniques of the BNS. The BNS offers an opportunity to be part of the mixture of people in New York City. It is helping my kids to develop tolerance and appreciation for all kinds of people and experiences.

My first goal for my child has already been met—she loves coming to school. She comes home skipping and singing and it's a great testimony to the school.

My child is very curious and inquisitive. This school provides that for her and I am happy with the results. When she's sick, she doesn't want to miss school.

Parent Committees

Parent committees that focus on specific issues or tasks are a way to reach out and involve a wide range of people who might not otherwise get involved. A committee structure at the Bronx New School maximizes family input into school functions. At different points in the school's history, different committees have been active. Among those that have existed are: a parent newsletter committee (described above), a fund-raising and finance committee (responsible for events like plant sales, book fairs, square dances, annual sales of a calendar featuring the children's artwork, holiday potlucks and tree and wreath sales, and so on), an after-school programs committee, an archives committee, a personnel committee (participating in the hiring of new staff), and a program committee to develop school educational and entertainment events. This last group has, over the years, planned and carried out such activities as a household-item drive for homeless people, a series of workshops on health education/family living, family trips, spring fairs, a *Brown versus Board of Education* celebration, end-of-year holiday parties/la Casa Boriqua, staff luncheons, CPR workshops, school picnics, and end-of-year celebrations/staff presentations.

In the early years of the school, when a new site was needed to accommodate the expanding population, even though the Board of Education (as it was then called) was responsible for finding the new site and overseeing its renovations, a parent committee was set up to oversee the project. Leading this committee was a parent who was an architect. He shepherded the process from search to lease signing, building design, permits, and construction. After drawing plans for the new building, he made sure to elicit input from the children, staff, and families of the school. His first draft was put up in the school office where anyone could come in to review it and post comments about it. After the revised draft was submitted to the Board of Education and the renovation finally began, he visited regularly to make sure that everything proceeded smoothly. Sometimes he took along a class from the school so that the children could see how the construction was progressing.

Parents in committees also took initiative when the first cohort of children at the Bronx New School was nearing middle-school age. Then, a parent committee worked with the Board of Education to set up a new middle school that would extend the teaching philosophy and practices into upper grades. (This group was eventually successful. They created the Jonas Broncks Academy, a separate public school for sixth to eighth graders that is in a neighboring Bronx community.)

EFFORTS TO MAXIMIZE FAMILY INVOLVEMENT

Right from the beginning, parents at the Bronx New School played an active role in promoting, strengthening, and supporting parent involvement in the everyday life of the school. Those who took the lead in the early days of the school asked a lot of questions: What are the needs of families? How do we identify those needs? What encourages/ discourages parents to voice their concerns, to get involved? Given the racial and class diversity in the school, how do we ensure that families from less wealthy communities who have fewer political connections and experiences and less formal education, people of color, and single-parent households will be able to fully participate? What role can we play in supporting the staff and in promoting unity throughout the school community?

Representatives from the parent committees first met at monthly steering committee meetings where implementation issues were discussed and decided. Decisions about matters of general policy were then made at monthly general parent meetings. A few years later, when the state made a policy that all schools should have a school leadership team, the existing leadership committee of the school (made up of only parents and the director) was expanded to include teachers as well. Working in this way over the years has provided an outlet for the expression of many people's ideas, offering parents opportunities to think about and explore new roles and relationships. In doing this they model for children how adults can engage with powerful ideas and act on them in powerful ways.

CHALLENGES TO INCREASED INVOLVEMENT

The benefits of increased family involvement in a school do not come without challenges. Because the involvement of families in most schools has traditionally been confined to arenas peripheral to educational matters, when families *do* get a chance to have more access and input into the educational life of a school, confusion, uncertainty, and difficulties can arise because this is such unfamiliar territory. Parameters of power may not be clear and, as a result, boundaries and roles can get blurred. Finding the right balance between parents' and educators' roles in determining educational philosophy, teaching methods, curriculum development, and personnel practices is not easy.

Some of the questions that have been struggled with to find this balance at the Bronx New School have been the following: To what degree should parents have input into curricular decisions and teaching methods? What should be done if parents don't like some of the teaching methods used in the school? What role should parents have in decisions about school organizational structures? To what extent should parents be involved in hiring and other personnel issues? While in most traditional schools these questions generally do not arise because the responsibilities of administrators, teachers, and parents are clearly delineated and demarcated, because parents made many decisions during the Bronx New School's founding years, these questions have presented themselves time and again.

As families and staff have struggled over the years to work through these issues and find the right balance, the multiple forums for expression of their views that have been described in this chapter have helped to hash out differences, develop new insights, solidify connections, and strengthen relationships. While the road has been bumpy at times, what has helped ease the process has been the strong presence of the school's foundational values. When differences have surfaced about teaching (such as about what methods are most effective at teaching reading or math) or about class configurations (for example, whether to have multiage or single-grade classes), everyone has referred to the principles on which the school was founded to guide decisions about what to do.

It is a given that change is hard. Moving toward the unknown can create anxieties and uncertainties. But from the educators' perspective, one thing I know for sure is that whatever decisions or changes need to be made about the practices of a school, it is incumbent on the educators who want to make them to explain their views thoroughly to the families in their community so that plans and actions are well understood, connect to shared values, and make sense to all. Only by doing this will the educators' actions have any chance of garnering the community's support.

While the particularities of the Bronx New School are unique, the tensions experienced between families and educators throughout the years of its existence are challenges faced by *any* school community that tries to nurture strong home-school partnerships and seeks to engage in renewal and change. Finding a way to work through the process requires lots of avenues for communication and involvement. Strong leadership is also needed to ensure that everyone's views are aired and listened to and that the community is steered toward consensus about what should be done. The critical role of leadership in building and sustaining a strong learner-centered community is explored next.

CHAPTER 11

Building Leadership for Learning

The need for leadership in the struggle to improve schools has been the subject of much discussion and many reports (Fullan, 2008; Lieberman & Miller, 2004; Sergiovanni, 2004). Leadership influences how schools can change, how new ways of working can be established, and how norms can be "built into the walls" of a school through the subtle interchanges of everyday life.

By examining the experiences and understandings of the leaders and teacher-leaders who are (or have been) at the Bronx New School, this chapter seeks insights to such questions as, What kinds of norms and structures support educators in a school to engage in and assume leadership for learning? How are these built and sustained? How does leadership uphold and enact core values of the school community? How does leadership balance competing demands from both external and internal forces in the school? What other challenges are involved in leadership of a school that focuses on teaching in the ways that children learn?

VIEWING EVERYONE AS A LEARNER AND LEADER

At the Bronx New School all the members of the school community—students, staff, and families alike—are viewed as learners and provided with continual growth opportunities. Just as students and families are encouraged to exchange ideas between themselves and with the teachers (through small-group discussions, class meetings, and meetings of the whole school community), teachers and other school support staff also have various opportunities for ongoing learning. Staff members meet together in formal as well as informal meetings where ideas and resources are exchanged to deepen understandings of their students, their teaching, and their own learning.

Facilitating these continual ways in which members of the school community connect and reconnect is the job of the school leader.

Throughout the history of the Bronx New School, the leadership role has consistently been to create an atmosphere that is respectful, trusting, and enabling of the learning of the children and adults involved. When I was the leader of the Bronx New School, I wanted to create for the adults the same kind of learning environment we wanted for the children: one based on nurturing the ways people learn and providing continual opportunities for everyone's growth and development. All involved in the school's creation worked to set up structures and processes to do this. To begin this chapter, I describe these structures and processes for professional learning, explaining how they have evolved and how they have affected those involved. Then I focus on salient aspects of the leadership role and the challenges that role presents.

STRUCTURES AND PROCEDURES
FOR PROFESSIONAL LEARNING

A description of how some staff procedures have become institutionalized into the life of the school illuminates some interesting dynamics about organizational growth and the evolution of a community.

Meetings

Since its inception, meetings have occupied an important place in the life of the Bronx New School—meetings for teachers, for children, and for families. Recognizing the importance of these gatherings to create the shared meanings and coherence that characterize a professional culture, the school to this day continues a schedule to ensure that a variety of regular meetings are held for the staff.

Teacher and Staff Meetings. Informal meetings provide some of the richest exchanges. They take place over lunch or in the many hours of coming to school early or staying late, when staff members chat together in hallways, clean their rooms, prepare materials, or photocopy homework assignments in the school's office.

Formal meetings take place in the form of weekly staff meetings or, occasionally, an all-school retreat. Like many of the activities in which the teachers take part, these meetings are not mandated by the union contract. Nevertheless, all the teachers commit themselves to attending as part of the responsibilities they accept when they join the school community. The meetings are divided between taking care of school business and discussing pedagogical issues.

In the early years of the school, many of the meetings were devoted to study of individual children through the *Descriptive Review* process; study of teaching through *curriculum reviews* and *reviews of practice* (Carini & Featherstone, 2001); and study of child development, literacy development, constructivist mathematics, and authentic assessment practices. Documents from the professional associations guided the development of goals and standards that were unique to the school. This early work built a strong foundation of coherent practice, which continues today, supported by ongoing staff discussions about many of the same topics.

Staff meetings also provide opportunities for teachers to share resources, to discuss questions regarding such matters as discipline, room arrangement, scheduling, record keeping, family communication, assessment/accountability, or issues pertaining to a particular child. Additionally, current issues and problems are often addressed—such as high-stakes testing, mandated curricula, class grouping structures, and community building. All those who work in the school attend, including the aides, the out-of-classroom teachers, and sometimes even the office administrative staff. This is done to emphasize the fact that educational issues are not the purview of just the head teachers. In fact, it is often these support staff members who raise important educational problems or issues. Because they see the children in the playground, informal conversations, and other social situations, they learn things about the children's strengths and personal nuances that might not appear in the more academic setting of the classroom. For example, an aide to a special needs child in one of the classes helped the whole staff heighten their sensitivity to children with special needs during a meeting devoted to looking at student work. His cautionary note that to evaluate children based on their test scores "unintentionally discriminates" against children who express their learning best in other ways challenged the teachers to more deeply pursue multiple ways of assessing what children know. It led to discussions that made everyone more conscious of how a teacher's own preferred modality may affect what and how he or she assesses and of how children need ways to express what they know that are complimentary to their own learning styles.

In addition to staff meetings, other structures at the Bronx New School enhance the staff's professional learning. Grade-level teams as well as cross-grade discipline-based committees meet regularly. To enable these groups to meet during the day instead of after school, when most teachers are exhausted, a permanent substitute works regularly in conjunction with specialty teachers (art, music, dance, drama, and so on) so that teachers can meet during the day. (This works because the staff does not have a large absentee problem, thus making the substitute available to cover classes.)

Grade-Level Teams. One of the main tasks of the grade-level team is to ensure that the teachers in the different classrooms work in sync with each other. Because the school formerly had multi-age classes (a class spanning two grades), which has now evolved into classes that loop (where children are in a single grade but stay with the same teacher for 2 years), this coordination is especially important. A major goal is to ensure that every child who progresses through the grades is exposed to the knowledge and skills outlined in the state and city standards.

Grade-level teams also serve as peer support for the teachers. They provide teachers with opportunities to exchange ideas and share teaching strategies and resources. At these meetings teachers discuss the details of what they are doing—what works, what doesn't, how to make sure that important content issues are being addressed. For example, one second-grade team whose meeting I sat in on was concerned about their students' reading comprehension skills. To work on this issue, the teachers on the team visited each other's classrooms to observe each other's reading groups. This "fishbowl exercise" was followed by a group debriefing, in which they offered suggestions and comments about how to enhance their work. (The teachers managed to all visit at the same time by arranging coverage for their classes from the different specialty teachers. They did this at the end of the morning so that they could have time for their follow-up discussion during lunch.)

Another example of how grade-level teams help teachers to support each other's work is a series of meetings that I attended of the third-grade teachers whose discussions were focused on math. In these meetings the teachers asked each other questions that reflected dilemmas they had encountered in their teaching ("How many of your kids can count by 6s to 48? I worry that even though we've done all the activities, if I were to ask my kids to count by 6s they couldn't"), and colleagues shared stories of what happened in their classes, strategies they had used that were effective, and materials that were suited to the subject at hand. As the teachers shared ideas and talked about materials, one offered suggestions for how to make math games. Her colleagues bombarded her with questions: "What kind of oaktag did you use? Where can I get it? What thickness do I need? What colors?" The teacher who shared her experience with the games answered the questions of her colleagues, offering other little details about, for example, not laminating the pieces because, even though they don't last as long that way, they work better and are easier to pick up. She also recommended a book of assessments for mathematical thinking and invited others to drop by her classroom to see her work.

Cross-Grade Discipline-Based Committees. Cross-grade discipline-based committees are made up of representatives from each grade who work together to chart out a course of study across all the grades in a specific discipline area. Their job is to ensure continuity and coherence for that content area throughout the grades. Team members map out, in a general way, the standards and content areas they want each grade to address so that when children leave the school at the end of fifth grade they will have been exposed to the big ideas and the important skills of the state standards.

The Math Committee offers an interesting example of how cross-grade content area committees work. The group created benchmarks based on their expectations of what they wanted to hold themselves accountable to and then mapped these back to the state and city standards. Committee members then hashed out how to manage the development of curricula for each grade, eventually bringing the plans they developed back to their grade-level teams for more work. By means of this process, teachers throughout the school revised and refined their goals and gained a solid grasp of areas of their teaching that needed to be strengthened. The Math Committee, like other discipline-based committees, documented their evolving curriculum in binders, ensuring that those who enter the school in the future will have resources to continue this work. Documenting in this way builds a living history of the teaching/learning life of the school.

Staff Developers and In-School Coaches

In recent years, the New York City Department of Education has recognized the importance of ongoing professional development by funding a mathematics and literacy coach in each school of each district. Before this happened, however, the Bronx New School already had these positions, supported by funds solicited through grants. Over the years, these staff developers have observed and modeled in classrooms, offering teachers another perspective on how to teach and another pair of eyes to reflect on their work. They sometimes also provide support for teachers to do research about their own practice.

For example, the literacy staff developer goes into classrooms to model how to do a running record (an observational assessment of children's reading in which the teacher notes patterns of errors children make so that they gain insight to what children know and the strategies they use to make meaning out of text). Afterward, in a conference with the teachers, the staff developer explains what she did and why she did it. She then asks the teachers what they noticed, questioning and probing them in much the same way that she would want them to do with their students.

Another staff developer works with a grade-level team in an after-school meeting to help them "level" their libraries (sorting, labeling, and arranging classroom library books according to their difficulty level so that children who are at different stages of development can know which books are "just right" for them). As the teachers and staff developer review and discuss children's texts in this way, they gain a deeper understanding of how to support their students' literacy learning.

Whether the staff developer is a school "insider" (someone who is part of the staff), someone from the district, or someone from an outside organization (from the Teachers College Reading and Writing Project, for example) the focus in staff development is on keeping everybody up to date on teaching strategies and on delving more deeply into practice so that all continue to grow into ever more thoughtful, more expert practitioners.

Other Professional Learning Opportunities

Other learning opportunities for continuous professional growth are conferences, workshops, and courses that teachers attend outside school as well as visits they make to other schools. Sometimes everyone reads the same article or book and then discusses it together as a way of processing new ideas. No matter which structure or process is used, however, each one of the experiences described above exemplifies the ongoing co-learning that is at the heart of professional development in a school that strives to be a community of learners.

TEACHERS TAKING THE LEAD

In a learning community that thrives and endures, the individuals involved have continual opportunities to "outgrow themselves" in both personal and professional ways. Not only are there numerous avenues to be exposed to new skills and ideas, there are also various ways for people to take the lead in dealing with the problems and challenges that come up in the school (Barth, 2003). At the Bronx New School these kinds of opportunities to exercise leadership are provided for everyone—both novice and experienced teachers. As teachers critically evaluate theirs and their colleagues' work, problem-solve issues, and articulate ideas and understandings to others, they create rather than merely apply knowledge, acting as agents for improvement and change. A few images, described below, give a sense of what this looks like.

Defending Pedagogy in the Face of Mandates

When the New York City Department of Education a few years ago mandated that all elementary schools in the city adopt the same mathematics program, teachers at the Bronx New School were not happy. They had just completed a multiyear project of articulating their own expectations for students in mathematics that were based on a different curriculum that they felt was better suited to how children learn. They had mapped out the curriculum to have coherence throughout the grades, to fit nicely into the looping (2-year sequence) pattern of their classrooms, and to align with city and state standards. Activities had been designed, materials had been collected, and lots of details for implementation had been worked out. All this had been documented in binders and explained to school families through meetings, workshops, and articles that the teachers themselves had developed. In an effort to protect this work from the citywide mandate, teachers took the lead in making an appeal, to their district supervisor, regional superintendent, and even the city's chancellor of education, garnering support from school families and local educational leaders. Although the appeal was not granted, the teachers' activism demonstrated their commitment to and knowledge of their pedagogy as well as their ability to explain their values and practice to others. While disappointed that their work was not recognized by the "powers that be," they persevered to figure out how to incorporate all that they had done in the past into the new format they were required to follow.

Maintaining Values in the Midst of Change

Another example of teacher leadership at the Bronx New School comes from the time, mentioned in earlier chapters, when the school shifted from multi-age to single-grade classes. Despite mixed feelings about this change, all the teachers (even those who were opposed) played a leadership role in problem solving how to make sure that the values of heterogeneity and community would stay alive in the new structure. They met together to organize the new configurations to ensure the classes would be heterogeneously mixed; to "loop" the classes so that children would have the benefit of staying with the same teacher for 2 years; to reconfigure grade-level teams to ensure that they would still be able to support each other and provide continuity between and among the grades; and to set up cross-grade curriculum projects, inter-age mentoring, and all-school meetings to ensure that children in the school could still experience what it is like to live in a school that is a community of learners.

Leading from the Classroom

As can be seen from these examples, leadership in a school isn't exclusive to the role of the principal or director and doesn't mean that teachers who want to exercise leadership must leave the classroom to do so. Rather, it can be exercised by many—through the force of ideas well articulated and the power of exemplary practice. Ronnie, the kindergarten teacher featured in an earlier chapter of this book, was such a teacher leader. Her years of experience and her wealth of knowledge about young children and teaching made her a sought-after candidate for "official" leadership positions. But she loved working in the classroom and didn't want to leave. It was her involvement with the children that fed her emotionally and it was through her work with them that she built her knowledge about teaching and learning. She chose to stay in the classroom. To the credit of the leaders she worked with over the years, she was able to exercise *her* leadership by playing an active role in school teams, committees, and meetings; by mentoring new teachers and other school personnel; and by helping develop school families' understandings about education. "What made the difference for me about staying in the classroom," Ronnie once told me, "was the structures for sharing that exist in the school."

Leading in the Profession and the World Beyond School

Ronnie, like other teachers at the Bronx New School, also exercised leadership in the world outside school. Based on the extensive documentation that she did of her teaching and the children's learning in her classroom, she wrote about it, presented at conferences, and made several videos of her teaching. Other teachers in the school have exerted leadership as well. For example, Martha, whose Colonial New York curriculum I described in Chapter 6, is featured in the Carnegie Foundation's *Inside Teaching* Web-based video collection of exemplary teaching (http://www.tc.columbia.edu/ncrest/teachers/andrews/). Other teachers have participated in the school's leadership structures—the Personnel Committee or the School Leadership Team. Still others have worked with citywide organizations in support of the values and practices they hold dear. For example, when New York City instituted a new policy of retaining all third graders whose performance on the citywide test did not meet the required standard, some of the Bronx New School teachers attended meetings and hearings, speaking out about the dangers of using only one form of evidence to make important decisions about children's lives. And most recently, other Bronx New School teachers, in an effort to extend the school's values and practices to other neighboring Bronx communities, joined together to create and lead a new charter elementary school.

These examples demonstrate how a school can be organized for teachers to learn together and take the lead. As teachers question assumptions, pose problems, and discuss dilemmas together, they continually refine and deepen their practice. This kind of growth is valued deeply by teachers, as expressed in this comment that Ronnie shared with me: "The conversations and dialogue we have together as a staff are the most important thing for me. We grow because we share."

It is through such sharing and ongoing conversations about ideas, concerns, processes, and values that a school's outlook and philosophy evolve. It is also how professional growth takes place, posing a reconceptualized model of professional development, one that is not about "training" teachers to passively implement programs brought in by "experts" who are assumed to know all the answers, but rather, one that enables teachers to be active constructors of knowledge derived from their own practice. When teachers tap into that knowledge, share it with others, and connect it with understandings from other venues, they develop both personally and professionally. This process can be powerful, especially when it is rooted in the particularities of the needs and understandings of those involved. Under these conditions, a teacher's learning need never end.

THE LEADER: BALANCING CHALLENGES AND COMMITMENTS

The leadership role in a school is critical for supporting teachers' continual growth. It is also critical for creating a climate in which everyone—not only teachers but children and families as well—is able to learn and to grow.

Facilitating Other People's Learning

Through my experience being the Bronx New School's leader, I came to understand that good leadership practice is much the same as good teaching in a classroom. I learned that leadership is about valuing each person's different gifts and strengths and then finding a way to help that person use them; that it is about trying to figure out where each person is in his or her practice and what supports can be given to them to attend to their needs; and that to do this effectively involves offering empathy, partnership, and understanding so that each individual develops enough of a sense of safety and belonging to take the risks that are needed to truly learn.

Paul, the current principal of the Bronx New School, believes this too. In an interview I had with him, he spoke of how he tries to support teacher growth:

> I try to recognize everyone's strengths. I try to work from peoples' strengths and differentiate the expectations of what they are to do. Teachers get stale if you do not respect their special needs— those of the senior as well as the novice teacher.

Paul builds on strengths by doing things like moving a classroom teacher who is having difficulties out of the classroom to teach a special subject in her area of strength or by helping a master teacher who does not want to leave the classroom find a way to play a leadership role with his or her colleagues. The goal is not only to provide for everyone's differing needs, but also to help everyone be a lifelong learner and to create a community of learning in the school. Paul elaborated further:

> I want to help people want to keep being learners, to never settle and always get better at their practice. People are thinkers and growers if given the opportunity. When the Bronx New School was first put together, the folks involved wanted to do better things for children. The people who came here to teach took time to look for a place that fit their style and was where they wanted to be. The people here now are also always looking for ways to learn. That's why they stay late and work hard. I try to assist them by treating them in the same way that I want them to treat the kids they teach. I want them to work from children's strengths, look for their successes, and always try to get the most from them.

There are many ways that leaders can help deepen and sustain teachers' individual and collective learning. They can encourage experienced teachers to "stay fresh"—try out new ideas, teach a different grade level, learn new technologies, attend classes or conferences, or teach with other colleagues. They can also help orient new teachers to learner-centered thinking and support them to develop effective teaching strategies. This can be done by using existing resources creatively as well as by seeking additional outside resources to provide supports for the kinds of learning opportunities described above: visits to others' classrooms, trips to other schools, grade-level teams and cross-grade committee meetings, group discussions of professional books and articles, and meetings on issues of common concern. Activities like these continually engage teachers and staff in talk about ideas, values, processes, and concerns. Such conversations develop collegiality, collaboration, and community.

Supporting teachers in these ways challenges leaders to find the right balance between push and support—to push to help teachers (and children) become "all they can be" in a way that nurtures their strengths and builds their capacities. I struggled with this challenge as a leader. Paul, the Bronx New School's current principal, does too. He expressed our joint sentiments about the challenge this way:

> Sometimes I have to say, "You have to do more; it's not good enough." We have to let kids know what standards are and push them so that they can reach their potentials. I am convinced we can do this without compromising our core values of supporting the development of the whole child.

Challenging each individual to work toward his or her personal standard of excellence requires pushing people to go outside their comfort zone. But it must be done with sensitivity, empathy, and care and in the context of the school's commitment to its values. At the Bronx New School this commitment has always meant keeping the child at the center of the work. The school leader's job has always been to keep reminding everyone of this fact. To keep focused and true to this value, the school's different leaders have spent time engaging directly with the children—talking and listening to them, helping them learn how to work together. This kind of involvement was one of the favorite parts of my job as a school leader. I took on the responsibilities of overseeing the buses, breakfast, lunch, and recess, for leading the weekly all-school meeting, and for working individually with several struggling learners. Paul, the current principal, involves himself with the children too. He is a constant presence in the school corridors and classrooms and works regularly with a small group of children in a book club. Being "in the company of children" he says, is what helps him get up in the morning and continue to come to school each day.

Balancing Roles

In addition to providing the resources and supports to encourage ongoing professional learning, leading a school community focused on and committed to teaching the way children learn involves other challenges that are both internal and external.

In the course of their daily lives in schools, leaders experience many situations that challenge their values, question their commitments, and test their educational understandings. They are called upon to simultaneously be educators, problem solvers, crisis managers, change agents, enablers, consensus builders, networkers, limit setters, and authority figures. Balancing these roles requires figuring out when to assert and when to hold back; when to intervene and how to do it right; when to deliberately lead and take a position and when to facilitate group struggle; how to handle conflict and make it productive; how to be accepting and respectful of differences while seeking to achieve overall agreement; how to be patient and supportive of strengths in the face of difficult problems; how to nurture teachers' growth in the right balance between push and support; how to simultaneously advocate for teachers, children, and their families while maintaining the day-to-day functioning of a school.

Upholding the Core Values of the School

As the years have gone by and the school has evolved, a major challenge for Bronx New School leaders has been the preservation of the core values: a belief that all children can learn, a respect for diversity, teaching practices that support the active nature of children's learning, and a concern about nurturing the "whole child." As the school has grown in size and brought in new people, leaders have also had to work to find ways to maintain the original school community's intimacy and zeal. This has entailed developing ways to avoid insularity, self-satisfaction, and nonproductive conflict as well as creating mechanisms to connect to ideas and people in the outside world.

Another challenge that has arisen as the school has become more established is how to keep the cohesiveness of the original community from becoming diluted. Other small schools have experienced this problem too. As many have become increasingly successful, their population has changed. Families have joined the schools for a variety of reasons. Some come in search of a child-centered philosophy, for others the educational philosophy doesn't matter as much as the fact that the school simply has a "good" reputation or that it is safe and well-equipped or that it has a caring staff.

Such a diversity of reasons for attending a school also brings diverse views about future directions and priorities. Sometimes teachers or families who actually have conflicts with the school's fundamental values end up being a part of the community. This presents an important challenge to school leadership—a challenge to educate and build a base of support for child-centered practices while being respectful of input and participation that seems contrary to this goal. Listening, evaluating, and responding to concerns in a way that incorporates professional knowledge about teaching and change are some of the ways to address this challenge. One memorable example of this for me was when a parent objected to heterogeneous grouping out of a belief that it didn't best serve her child. She wanted the school to reconsider this practice and change to classes and groupings organized around ability levels. I had to find a way to help her understand that this value was foundational to the school and would remain inviolable.

Keeping the school's vision alive is not easy. It necessitates being aware that although one has the power to "push things through," it is not worth it. Instead, connecting to what people understand, want, believe, and are ready to do is the real challenge. This involves understanding that having a good idea or being right is just simply not enough. The leader's job is to help others embrace good ideas, come together to create a common vision around them, and then work jointly to enact that vision.

How to be a hub and be central to all aspects of the school while not dominating, how to speak for all the constituencies without demanding compliance to a singular view, and how to turn problems into possibilities are also important aspects of leadership. Creating these conditions calls on leaders to remain open to change and to connect closely to all aspects of school life. It also requires stepping back sometimes in the heat of differences in order to be able to mediate and move the community forward.

Another challenge inherent in the leadership role (and this, I am sure, is not just unique to schools) is how to manage negative reactions to the leadership role itself, especially reactions that seem unwarranted. I remember feeling sometimes that people were not talking or reacting to me, but rather that they were talking or reacting to "the principal." It almost didn't matter what I said; I was in the role of the authority figure and it affected all interchanges with others. How not to take this personally and, instead, rise above it, reframe differences, and mediate conflict are important continual challenges of leadership in a school or any setting.

All these examples represent leadership challenges that regularly appear in school life. When a leader is able to deal with them effectively, everyone in a school learns and grows.

Mediating External Challenges and Demands

While the internal growth of a school community presents challenges that pull a leader in different directions, problems of the outside world call for a related yet different set of skills. In the midst of these challenges, the primary responsibility of a school leader is, once again, to protect the foundational values of the school. This involves negotiating the demands of the outside world with the inside world of the school culture, which often involves being a buffer between the teachers, the families, the district, and the world at large. The challenge is to instill in everyone a larger vision that transcends the demands of both worlds and to protect as well as create school structures and practices that nurture the holistic development of all (students, their families, and the school's teachers).

In recent years, protecting this work has become ever more difficult because of the mandates and high-stakes policies that have been imposed on today's public schools. District, state, and federal policies as well as both local and national politics are often in conflict with the school's values. Curriculum mandates, standardized testing, and retention practices clash directly with the developmental and holistic practices that are fundamental to teaching the way children learn. While teaching and assessment within a school like the Bronx New School are geared to the differing strengths and needs of students, the success of the school and its practices is nevertheless measured almost solely through the use of standardized tests, known to do a notoriously poor job of reflecting students' strengths and differences (Darling-Hammond, 2006; Falk, 2000; Shepard, 2002). This phenomenon places the leadership in a school such as the Bronx New School in an inextricable bind. The leader must help educators simultaneously fulfill requirements for survival in the established system while struggling to develop and maintain an alternate stance that refuses to allow categorization of students, fragmentation of the school program, and a standardized conception of learning to take hold.

An example of how these tensions play out for the leader is the restructuring of classrooms from multi-age to looped same-grade classes that was discussed earlier. Paul advocated for this change because he felt it was the best way to meet the pressures of imposed curricula, testing, and retention policies. He argued that moving to single-grade classes would not only help the children meet district demands; instituting looping combined with across-grade projects would still ensure that children could be well known by their teachers as well as maintain the sense of community so valued by the school. Adopting this position was Paul's way of upholding the founding values of the school in the context of the demands of current policies. As he explained: "My main concern is that the good work we do here connects to results that the district understands. At the same time I want to work to change the system so that it better supports what we do here. All I want is to do what's best for the children. But to do this, I need to use different ways—different from the ways of the school district administration and different from some of the ways of the school's past."

Of course, only time will be the judge of this strategy. Ultimately, safeguarding the collective values of the school calls for a keen sense of strategy that involves the ability to understand what is essential, communicate ideas effectively, and balance the strengths of the past with the demands of the present.

REFRAMING LEADERSHIP

In many ways the leadership challenges at the Bronx New School are much like the challenges faced in other schools trying to deal with changing student and parent populations and with the integration of new knowledge and approaches to learning and assessment. Indeed, the qualities discussed here are qualities that much of the research on leadership has pointed to as being effective. What distinguishes the images of leadership described here, however, is the way it supports the core values of the community as well as enables the work and ideas of others.

In the traditional school, the leader is assumed to be the fount of pedagogical knowledge as well as the repository of power and control over all resources, both human and material. The principal is the figure of authority that all accede to, whose mission is to run an orderly and technically tight organization. While no one would dispute the need for an orderly and well-run school, what distinguishes the paradigm of leadership discussed here, exhibited in these examples from the Bronx New School, is that it enables rather than controls others. It seeks to build the capacities of school community members, including them in decisions that are critical to their lives and their work. Leadership enacts the ideals that the community embraces, recognizing that the work is never finished but is "continually in the making" (Lieberman & Falk, 2007, p. 1).

CHAPTER 12

Of Courage, Hope, and Possibility

My story began on a personal note. It continues today in my efforts to support new educators to teach in the ways children learn. But it continues also in the lives of all those who seek to create contexts that enable children to develop their capacities and realize their potentials. Despite the constraints of current policies, there are many courageous people who continue to struggle to make public education effective so that all children, regardless of the community they live in, the color of their skin, the language of their heritage, their gender or socioeconomic status, can gain access to fulfilling and productive lives. To those who embrace this daunting challenge, I reach back to my personal experiences one more time to sum up the lessons I have learned.

Perhaps the best way to begin is to share what I told a group of educators and parents of a soon-to-be-opened, newly created school, who recently approached me for advice. They asked: "What should we do? What problems should we look out for? What would you do again and what would you *not* do again if you were to lead another school?" Here is my response.

REVISIONING SCHOOLING TO SUPPORT DIVERSE LEARNERS

Teaching the way children learn is a way of thinking about children, families, educators, and learning that is manifested throughout the actions and attitudes of a school. This way of thinking is present not only in classroom curricula and teaching practices, but also in assessment systems, school structures and policies, home-school partnerships, leadership, and the values embedded within them all. To me, a school organized to teach the way children learn does the following:

- Creates meaningful and purposeful contexts for learning (within which is embedded explicit attention to important content and skills);

- Engages children in active experiences that build on their interests and use their strengths for the purpose of developing their deep understandings;
- Integrates the curriculum to enable children to make connections between ideas;
- Expects and supports everyone to develop the ability to think critically, to investigate and evaluate ideas, to be respectful of the perspectives of others, and to communicate and defend their thoughts orally and in writing;
- Is respectful of and responsive to diversity;
- Creates a community of care that pays attention to all aspects (social, emotional, physical, and cognitive) of the "whole child";
- Assesses children's learning through multiple measures that inform instruction and support children's learning;
- Involves families meaningfully in the life of the school;
- Is led by educators who build community, nurture professional collaboration, and place children's needs at the center of school life.

There is no one right way to create such a school. Those who pursue this important work must discover their own pathway to it, using their intelligence and creativity to shape what they do in response to the particularities of their context. There are a few non-negotiables, however. Above all, the one I hold to most firmly is that the context needs to be a community of care, manifested in the details that constitute the quality of school life: adults who listen and respond to children carefully, as seen through the tone of voice and gestures they use as they interact with children, their families, and each other; through daily routines that are conducted in a respectful manner, as seen in the atmosphere at breakfast/lunch/recess and when lining up for buses; the way security guards and custodians interact with students; how children who are challenging, troubled, lonely, or ill are treated by the adults entrusted to their care. A caring community is also evidenced by careful attention to aspects of children's lives traditionally not considered part of a school's responsibilities: after-school care, child care during meetings, help to families in making arrangements for children to attend extracurricular activities, information and resources that assist families with their needs.

Ultimately, a school that is a caring community and that teaches the way children learn creates an environment in which children are visible and well known for their strengths as well as needs. It instills in each child a sense of purpose, an ability to see the world in terms of what is possible, and a hope for a better tomorrow. Creating such an environment can be especially powerful for children from historically underserved communities, whose futures as successful learners have too often been compromised by low expectations and poorly qualified, unstable teaching. For such children, being in a community of care that teaches the way they learn is critical because it can offset the limited expectations that have been previously held out for them. At the same time, being in such a school can bolster *all* children's sense of self-worth, propelling them to learn, indeed even dream, in ways they may never before have imagined.

PROBLEMS AS OPPORTUNITIES TO LEARN

In the course of the work to revision schools, many problems and challenges will continually arise. In the sometimes confusing midst of these, it is important to remember that problems are intrinsic to the process; they are an inevitable part of making change. While it is easy to see a problem as a failure, especially for the person who is in the middle of struggling with it, the key to moving forward is to embrace it—as an opportunity to learn. To do this requires staying focused on one's values, persevering when a stumbling block appears, to find another way to get to the goal. Just as when water cascades down a mountain it flows over and around the boulders in its path, to move forward requires searching for a way around and over the encountered difficulties. It also requires exploring new approaches when something doesn't work, seeking common ground with those who have differences, and trying to build consensus with one's community of fellow change makers. Working in this way, step by step, one foot in front of the other, a solution will inevitably be found.

As I reflect on the stories recounted here, my efforts to improve schooling have come full circle. My daughters, the source of my inspiration, are both now grown and educators themselves. My work and theirs fill me with hope and make me more certain than ever that anything is possible, if there is the will. Just as the actions I took with my community years ago made a difference in the lives of many, I know that the efforts we will make in the future, along with the work of others who care, have the potential to make a difference too. Whether the goal is to get better at teaching, change a structure or policy, or even create a brand new school, to those who desire to do so I offer these last few words of advice: Don't wait for someone else to do it for you. As the ancient Hopi saying goes, "We are the ones we have been waiting for."

And while what you do may feel, at times, too hard or as if it is simply a leap of faith, bear in mind that

> hope calls for a leap of faith that goes "beyond the evidence to create new possibilities based on visions that become contagious." These visions . . . allow people to engage in "heroic actions, always against the odds, no guarantee whatsoever." (Anna Deveare Smith, quoting Cornel West, in Smith, 2006, pp. 5–6)

Whether you take a leap of faith or simply a few small steps forward, try to remember that nothing is perfect: there is no such thing as a perfect teacher, a perfect school, or a perfect change. Instead, all we can ask of ourselves is to give our best efforts to what we do. The seeds of tomorrow are in our actions today.

So as you go forth with your agenda for change, I hope that the images presented in this book are a useful guide for the challenges ahead.

There is so much work that needs to be done!

Just imagine the possibilities!

References

Adoff, A. (2004). *Black is brown is tan*. New York: Amistad.

American Association for the Advancement of Science. (1993). *Benchmarks for science literacy*. Oxford: Oxford University Press.

Association for Supervision and Curriculum Development. (2007). *The learning compact redefined: A call to action*. Washington, DC: Author.

Au, W. (2007). High-stakes testing and curricular control: A qualitative meta-synthesis. *Educational Researcher, 36*(5), 258–267.

Au, K., & Jordan, C. (1981). Teaching reading to Hawaiian children: Finding a culturally appropriate solution. In H. Tureba, G. Guthrie, & K. Au (Eds.), *Culture and the bilingual classroom: Studies in classroom ethnography* (pp. 139–152). Rowley, MA: Newbury House.

Ballenger, C. (1998). *Teaching other people's children: Literacy and learning in a bilingual classroom*. New York: Teachers College Press.

Banks, J. (2006). *Race, culture, and education: The selected works of James A. Banks*. New York: Routledge.

Barrs, M., Ellis, S., Hester, H., & Thomas, A. (1990). *The primary language record*. Portsmouth, NH: Heinemann.

Barth, R. (2003). *Lessons learned: Shaping relationships and the culture of the workplace*. Thousand Oaks, CA: Corwin.

Blythe, T. (1997). *Teaching for understanding*. San Francisco: Jossey-Bass.

Bowman, B. T., Donovan, M. S., & Burns, M. S. (Eds.). (2001). *Eager to learn: Educating our preschoolers*. Washington, DC: National Academy Press.

Boyer, E. (1995). *The Basic School: A community for learning*. Princeton, NJ: Carnegie Foundation.

Bransford, J. D., Brown, A. L., & Cocking, R. R. (Eds.). (2000). *How people learn: Brain, mind, experience, and school*. Washington, DC: National Academy of Sciences.

Bredekamp, S., & Copple, C. (1997). *Developmentally-appropriate practice in early childhood programs*. Washington, DC: National Association for the Education of Young Children.

Brown, A. L., & Campione, J. C. (1996). Psychological theory and the design of innovative learning environments: On procedures, principles, and systems. In L. Schauble & R. Glaser (Eds.), *Innovations in learning: New environments for education* (pp. 289–325). Mahwah, NJ: Erlbaum.

Brown, A. L., & Reeve, R. A. (1987). Bandwidths of competence: The role of supportive contexts in learning and development. In L. S. Liben (Ed.), *Development and learning: Conflict or congruence?* The Jean Piaget Symposium Series (pp. 173–223). Hillsdale, NJ: Erlbaum.

Bruner, J. (1966). *The process of education.* Cambridge, MA: Harvard University Press.

Bussis, A., Chittenden, E., Amarel, M., & Klausner, E. (1985). *Inquiry into meaning: An investigation of learning to read.* Hillsdale, NJ: Erlbaum.

Calkins, L. (1994). *The art of teaching writing.* Upper Saddle River, NJ: Allyn and Bacon.

Calkins, L. (2000). *The art of teaching reading.* Upper Saddle River, NJ: Allyn and Bacon.

Calkins, L., Santman, D., & Montgomery, K. (with Falk, B.) (1998). *A teacher's guide to standardized testing: Knowledge is power.* Portsmouth, NH: Heinemann.

Carini, P. (1986). Building from children's strengths. *Journal of Education, 168*(3), 13–24.

Carini, P. (1987). *On value in education.* New York: City College Workshop Center.

Carini, P., & Featherstone, J. (2001). *Starting strong: A different look at children, schools, and standards.* New York: Teachers College Press.

Carr, S. (2004, April 4). Blocks, nap time giving way to language and reading programs. *Milwaukee Journal Sentinel.* Retrieved October 20, 2007, from http://www.jsonline.com/story/index.aspx?id=219303

Cassie, R. (2006, August 31). SAT scores tied to income level locally, nationally. Examiner.com. Retrieved October 17, 2007, from http://www.examiner.com/a-254205~SAT_scores_tied_to_income_level_locally_nationally.html

Clay, M. (2007). *An observation survey of early literacy achievement* (Rev. ed.). Portsmouth, NH: Heinemann.

Cohen, D., McLaughlin, M., & Talbert, J. (Eds.). (1993). *Teaching for understanding: Challenges for policy and practice.* San Francisco: Jossey-Bass.

Comer, J., Haynes, N. M., Joyner, E. T., & Ben-Avie, M. (Eds.). (1999). *Rallying the whole village: The Comer process for reforming education.* New York: Teachers College Press.

Cremin, L. A. (1964). *The transformation of the school: Progressivism in American education, 1876–1957.* New York: Vintage.

Cummins, J. (2001). *Language, power, and pedagogy: Bilingual children in the crossfire.* Clevedon, UK: Multilingual Matters.

Darling-Hammond, L. (1991). The implications of testing policy for educational quality and equality. *Phi Delta Kappan, 73*(3), 220–225.

Darling-Hammond, L. (1997). *The right to learn: A blueprint for school reform.* San Francisco: Jossey-Bass.

Darling-Hammond, L. (2006). *Standards, assessments, and educational policy: In pursuit of genuine accountability.* Princeton, NJ: Educational Testing Service.

Darling-Hammond, L. (2007). Evaluating "No Child Left Behind." *The Nation.* Retrieved March 1, 2008, from http://www.forumforeducation.org/resources/index.php?item=357&page=27

Datnow, A., & Castellano, M. (1999, April). An "inside look" at the implementation of Success for All: Teachers' responses to the reform. Paper presented at the annual meeting of the American Educational Research Association, Montreal, Canada.

Delpit, L. (2002). The skin that we speak: Thoughts on language and culture in the classroom. New York: The New Press.

Delpit, L. (2006a). Lessons from teachers. Journal of Teacher Education, 57(3), 220–231.

Delpit, L. (2006b). Other people's children: Cultural conflict in the classroom (Updated ed.). New York: New Press.

Dewey, J. (1916). Democracy and education. New York: Macmillan.

Dewey, J. (1938). Education and experience. New York: Macmillan.

Dewey, J. (1956). The school and society. Chicago: University of Chicago Press. (Original work published 1900)

Du Bois, W. E. B. (1970). The freedom to learn. In P. S. Foner (Ed.), W. E. B. Du Bois speaks (pp. 230–231). New York: Pathfinder.

Duckworth, E. (1991). Twenty-four, forty-two, and I love you: Keeping it complex. Harvard Educational Review, 6(1), 1–24.

Duckworth, E. (2007). "The having of wonderful ideas" and other essays. New York: Teachers College Press. (Original work published 1987)

Elkind, D. (2001). Much too early. Education Next, 1(2), 9–15.

Epstein, J. (2002). School, family, and community partnerships: Your handbook for action (2nd ed.). Thousand Oaks, CA: Corwin.

Falk, B. (1994). The Bronx New School: Weaving assessment into the fabric of teaching and learning. New York: National Center for Restructuring Education, Schools, and Teaching.

Falk, B. (2000). The heart of the matter: Using standards and assessments to learn. Portsmouth, NH: Heinemann.

Falk, B. (2006, January 12). Morning meeting. ASCD Express, 1(7), Retrieved February 27, 2008, from http://www.ascd.org/

Falk, B., & Blumenreich, M. (2005). The power of questions: A guide to teacher and student research. Portsmouth, NH: Heinemann.

Falk, B., Ort, S., & Moirs, K. (2007). Keeping the focus on the child: Supporting and reporting on teaching and learning with a classroom-based assessment system. Educational Assessment, 12(1), 47–74.

Farnham-Diggory, S. (1990). Schooling: The developing child. Cambridge: Harvard University Press.

Feeney, S., Christensen, D., & Moravcik, E. (2005). Who am I in the lives of children? (7th ed.). Upper Saddle River, NJ: Prentice Hall.

Freire, P. (1971). Pedagogy of the oppressed. New York: Herder and Herder.

Fullan, M. (2008). What's worth fighting for in the principalship? (2nd ed.). New York: Teachers College Press.

Fuller, B., Wright, J., Gesicki, K., & Kang, E. (2007). Gauging growth: How to judge No Child Left Behind? Educational Researcher, 36, 268–278.

Gallagher, C. (2007). Reclaiming assessment. Portsmouth, NH: Heinemann.

Gao, H. (2005, April 11). Kindergarten or "kindergrind"? School getting tougher for kids. San Diego Union Tribune. Retrieved January 7, 2008, from www.signonsandiego.com/news/education/20050411-9999-1nllkinder.html

Garborino, J., Dubrow, N., Kostelny, K., & Pardo, C. (1998). *Children in danger: Coping with the consequences of community violence.* San Francisco: Jossey-Bass.

Gardner, H. (1983). *Frames of mind.* New York: Basic Books.

Gardner, H. (1991) *The unschooled mind: How children think, and how schools should teach.* New York: Basic Books.

Gardner, H. (1997). *Extraordinary minds: Portraits of exceptional individuals and an examination of our extraordinariness.* New York: Basic Books.

Gardner, H. (2006). *Multiple intelligences: New horizons.* Jackson, TN: Perseus Books Group.

Gay, G. (2000). *Culturally-responsive teaching: Theory, research, and practice.* New York: Teachers College Press.

Gibson, E. J. (1969). *Principles of perceptual learning and development.* New York: Appleton-Century-Crofts.

Good, R. H. & Kaminski, R. A. (2002). *DIBELS oral reading fluency passages for first through third grades* (Technical Report No. 10). Eugene: University of Oregon.

Goodman, K., Shannon, P., Goodman, Y., & Rappoport, R. (2004). *Saving our schools: The case for public education.* Muskegon, MI: RDR Books.

Graves, D. (2003). *Writing: Teachers and children at work* (20th anniversary ed.). Portsmouth, NH: Heinemann.

Greenberg, P. (1987). Lucy Sprague Mitchell: A major missing link between early childhood education in the 1980's and progressive education in the 1890's–1930's. *Young Children, 42*(5), 70–84.

Greene, M. (1978). *Landscapes of learning.* New York: Teachers College Press.

Greene, M. (1984). How do we think about our craft? *Teachers College Record, 86*(1), 55–67.

Hallam, R. N. (1970). Piaget and thinking in history. In M. Ballard (Ed.), *New movements in the study and teaching of history* (pp. 162–179). Bloomington: Indiana University Press.

Harlen, W. (2001). *Primary science: Taking the plunge.* Portsmouth, NH: Heinemann.

Hawkins, D. (1965). Messing about in science. *Science and Children, 2*(5), 5–9.

Hilliard, A. G. (2006). Aliens in the education matrix: Recovering freedom. *The New Educator, 2*(2), 87–102.

Hollins, E. R., King, J. E., & Hayman, W. C. (Eds.). (1994). *Teaching diverse populations: Formulating a knowledge base.* Albany: State University of New York Press.

Ingram, I., Seashore Louis, K. R., & Schroeder, R. (2004). Accountability policies and teacher decision making: Barriers to the use of data to improve practice. *Teachers College Record, 106*(6), 1258–1287.

Institute of Education Sciences. (2008). *Reading First impact study: An interim report.* (NCEE 2008-4016). Washington, DC: National Center for Education Evaluation and Regional Assistance, U.S. Department of Education.

International Reading Association & the National Council of Teachers of English. (1996). *Standards for the English language arts.* Newark, DE: Authors.

Jennings, J., & Rentner, D. S. (2006). Ten big effects of the No Child Left Behind Act on public schools. *Phi Delta Kappan, 88*(2), 110–113.

Jones, B. D., & Egley, R. J. (2004). Voices from the frontlines: Teachers' percep-
tions of high-stakes testing. *Education Policy Analysis Archives, 12*(39).
Retrieved December 18, 2007, from http://epaa.asu.edu/epaa/v12n39/

Kamii, C. (1985). *Young children reinvent arithmetic*. New York: Teachers College Press.

Katz, L. G., & Chard, S. C. (2000). *Engaging children's minds: The project approach* (2nd ed.). Toronto: Ablex.

Kohl, H. (1991). *I won't learn from you: And other thoughts on creative malad-
justment*. New York: The New Press.

Kozol, J. (1991). *Savage inequalities*. New York: Crown.

Krashen, S. D. (1996). *The natural approach: Language acquisition in the
classroom*. Northumberland, UK: Bloodaxe Books.

Krashen, S. (2007a). Did reading first work? Retrieved January 7, 2008, from
http://www.districtadministration.com/pulse/commentpost.aspx?news=
no&postid=173494

Krashen, S. (2007b). *NCLB: No impact on state fourth grade reading test
scores*. Retrieved December 21, 2007, from http://www.districtadministra-
tion.com/pulse/commentpost.aspx?news=no&postid=19497

Krashen, S. D., Tse, L., & McQuillan, J. (Eds.). (1998). *Heritage language development*. Burlingame, CA: Language Education Associates.

Ladson-Billings, G. (1994). *The dreamkeepers: Successful teachers of African-
American children*. San Francisco, CA: Jossey-Bass.

Ladson-Billings, G. (2005). *Culturally-relevant teaching*. Mahwah, NJ: Lawrence Erlbaum.

Lake, S. (2008, February 13). Paying for grades yields mixed results in boosting student achievement. *Diverse Issues in Higher in Education*. Retrieved
April 25, 2008, from http://www.diverseeducation.com/artman/publish/ar-
ticle_10648.shtml

Lave, J., & Wenger, E. (1991). *Situated learning: Legitimate peripheral participation*. New York: Cambridge University Press.

Lee, J. (2006). *Tracking achievement gaps and assessing the impact of NCLB
on the gaps: An in-depth look into national and state reading and math
outcome trends*. Cambridge, MA: Civil Rights Project.

Lieberman, A., & Falk, B. (2007). Leadership in learner-centered schools. In
A. Danzig, K. Borman, B. Jones, & W. Wright (Eds.), *Professional development for learner centered leadership: Policy, research, and practice*. Mahwah, NJ: Lawrence Erlbaum.

Lieberman, A., & Miller, L. (2004). *Teacher leadership*. San Francisco: Jossey-Bass.

MacDonald, C. (2005, March 13). It's all work, little play in kindergarten. *De-
troit News*.

Marshall, H. H. (1992). *Redefining student learning: Roots of educational
change*. Norwood, NJ: Ablex.

Martin, J. R. (1992). *The schoolhome: Rethinking schools for changing families*.
Cambridge, MA: Harvard University Press.

Martin-Kniep,G. (1998). *Why am I doing this? Purposeful teaching through
portfolio assessment*. Portsmouth, NH: Heinemann.

McNeil, L. (2000). *Contradictions of school reform: Educational costs of standardized testing.* London: Falmer.

Meier, D. (1991, September 23). Up against the system: The little schools that could. *The Nation,* pp. 1, 338–340.

Meier, D., & Wood, G. (Eds.). (2003). *Many children left behind: How the No Child Left Behind Act is damaging our children and our schools.* Boston: Beacon.

Meisels, S. J., Jablon, J. R., Marsden, D. B., Dichtelmiller, M. L., Dorfman, A. B., & Steele, D. M. (1995). *The work sampling system: An overview.* Ann Arbor, MI: Rebus Planning Associates.

Moll, L. (1995). Funds of knowledge for teaching in Latino households. *Urban Education, 9*(4), 443.

Moll, L. C., & Whitmore, K. (1993). Vygotsky in classroom practice: Moving from indidividual transmission to social transaction. In E. A. Forman, N. Minick, & C. A. Stone (Eds.), *Contexts for learning* (pp. 19–42). New York: Oxford University Press.

Moon, T. R., Callahan, C. M., & Tomlinson, C. A. (2003). Effects of state testing programs on elementary schools with high concentrations of student poverty—good news or bad news? *Current Issues in Education 6*(8). Retrieved March 30, 2008, from http://cie.ed.asu.edu/volume6/number8/

Morrison, S. (1991). Let me tell you about Harlem. *Family portraits: Stories in the oral tradition.* New York: The Bronx New School.

National Association for the Education of Young Children. (1987). *Standardized testing of young children 3 through 8 years of age.* Washington, DC: Author.

National Association for the Education of Young Children & National Association for Early Childhood Specialists in State Departments of Education. (2003). *Early childhood curriculum, assessment, and program evaluation.* Retrieved March 10, 2008, from http://www.naeyc.org/about/positions/pdf/pscape.pdf

National Association of School Psychologists. (2005). NASP position statement on early childhood assessment [Online document]. Bethesda, MD: NASP. Retrieved March 15, 2008, from http://www.nasponline.org/information/pospaper_eca.html

National Center for Education Statistics. (2004). *Highlights from the Trends in International Mathematics and Science Study (TIMSS) 2003.* Jessup, MD: U.S. Department of Education.

National Center for Restructuring Education, Schools, and Teaching. (2006). A fifth grade unit on Colonial New York: Developing perspectives through historic role play. Retrieved November 4, 2007, from http://gallery.carnegiefoundation.org/collections/quest/collections/sites/andrews_martha/

National Commission on Excellence in Education. (1983). *A nation at risk: The imperative for educational reform.* Washington, DC: U.S. Department of Education.

National Commission of Social Studies in the Schools. (1990). *Social studies for the 21st century.* Washington, DC: Author.

National Council of Teachers of Mathematics. (2000). *Principles and standards for school mathematics.* Reston, VA: Author.

New York Times. (1991, August 31). Schools and the mediocrity trap. Retrieved May 3, 2008, from http://query.nytimes.com/gst/fullpage.html?res=9D0CE 5DE1130F932A0575BC0A967958260

Newell, A., Shaw, J. C., & Simon, H. A. (1958). Elements of a theory of human problem solving. *Psychological Review, 65,* 151–166.

Newman, D., Griffin, P., & Cole, M. (1989). *The construction zone: Working for cognitive change in school.* New York: Cambridge University Press.

Nichols, S. L., Glass, G. V., & Berliner, D. C. (2005, September). *High stakes testing and student achievement: Problems with the No Child Left Behind Act.* Tempe, AZ: Education Policy Studies Laboratory.

Nieto, S. (1999). *Creating multicultural learning communities.* New York: Teachers College Press.

Noddings, N. (1984). *Caring: A feminine approach to ethics and moral education.* Berkeley and Los Angeles: University of California Press.

Noddings, N. (1992). *The challenge to care in schools.* New York: Teachers College Press.

Noddings, N. (2002). *Educating moral people: A caring alternative to character education.* New York: Teachers College Press.

Nolte, D. L., & Harris, R. (1972). *Children learn what they live.* Retrieved February 27, 2008, from http://www.empowermentresources.com/info2/childrenlearn.html

Osborne, R., & Freyberg, P. (1985). *Learning in science: The implications of children's science.* Portsmouth, NH: Heinemann.

Paulson, F. L., Paulson, P. R., & Meyer, C. A. (1991). What makes a portfolio a portfolio? *Educational Leadership, 48*(5), 60–63.

Perrone, V. (1991). *A letter to teachers: Reflections on schooling and the art of teaching.* San Francisco: Jossey-Bass.

Perry, T., & Delpit, L. (Eds.). (1998). *The real Ebonics debate: Power, language, and the education of African-American children.* Boston: Beacon.

Piaget, J. (1973). *To understand is to invent.* New York: Grossman.

Piaget, J. (1975). *The child's conception of the world.* Totowa, NJ: Littlefield, Adams.

Piaget, J. (1998). *The child's conception of space.* London: Routledge.

Piaget, J. (2000). *The psychology of the child.* New York: Basic.

Piaget, J., & Inhelder, B. (1969). *The psychology of the child.* New York: Basic.

Pinnell, G. S., & Fountas, I. (1996). *Guided reading: Good first teaching for all children.* Portsmouth, NH: Heinemann.

Pogrow. S. (2000). The unsubstantiated "success" of Success for All: Implications for policy, practice, and the soul of our profession. *Phi Delta Kappan, 81*(8), 596.

Popham, J. (2001). *The truth about testing: An educator's call to action.* Alexandria, VA: Association for Supervision and Curriculum Development.

Renyi, J. (1992, December 9). Lessons from lunch (and recess). *Education Week,* pp. 36, 28.

Resnick, L. B. (1987). *Education and learning to think.* Washington, DC: National Academy Press.

Richardson, E. (2003) *African American literacies,* New York: Routledge.

Rickford, J. R. (1999). *African American vernacular English: Features, evolution, educational implications.* Malden, MA: Blackwell.

Rogoff, B., & Wertsch, J. V. (Eds.). (1984). *Childrens' learning in the "Zone of Proximal Development."* San Francisco: Jossey-Bass.

Rogoff, G. (2003). *The cultural nature of human development.* Oxford: Oxford University Press.

Rothstein, R. (2004, November 2). Too young to test. *American Prospect, 15*(11). Retrieved February 7, 2007, from http://www.prospect.org/web/page.ww?section=root&name=ViewPrint&articleId=8774

Rousseau, J. (1762). *Emile.* New York: Dutton.

Sampson, R. J., Sharkey, P., & Raudenbush, S. W. (2007). Durable effects of concentrated disadvantage on verbal ability among African-American children. *PNAS Early Edition,* 1–8. Retrieved December 21, 2007, from http://www.pnas.org_cgi_doi_10.1073_pnas.0710189104

Sergiovanni, T. J. (2004). *The lifeworld of leadership: Creating culture, community, and personal meaning in our schools.* San Francisco: Jossey-Bass.

Shepard, L. A. (2002). Standardized tests and high-stakes assessment. In J. Guthrie (Ed.), *Encyclopedia of Education* (Vol. 6, 2nd ed., pp. 2533–2537). New York: Macmillan Reference.

Shonkoff, J. P., & Phillips, D. A. (Eds.). (2000). *From neurons to neighborhoods: The science of early childhood development.* Washington, DC: National Academy Press.

Shulman, L. (1987). Knowledge and teaching: Foundations of the new reform. *Harvard Educational Review, 57,* 1–22.

Siegel, D. (2001). *The developing mind: How relationships and the brain interact to shape who we are.* New York: Guilford.

Singer, D. G., & Singer, J. L. (1990). *The house of make-believe: Children's play and the developing imagination.* Cambridge, MA: Harvard University Press.

Sizer, T. R. (1984). *Horace's compromise: The dilemma of the American high school.* Boston: Houghton Mifflin.

Skinner, B. F. (1954). The science of learning and the art of teaching. *Harvard Educational Review, 24*(2), 86–97.

Smith, A. D. (2006). *Letters to a young artist.* New York: Anchor Books.

Smith, M. L. (1991). Put to the test: The effects of external testing on teachers. *Educational Researcher, 20*(5), 8–11.

Smitherman, G. (1977). *Talkin and testifyin: The language of Black America.* Boston: Houghton Mifflin.

Society for Research in Child Development. (2008, March 26). Family wealth may explain differences in test scores in school-age children. *Science Daily.* Retrieved April 25, 2008, from http://www.sciencedaily.com/releases/2008/03/080325083329.htm

Tatum, B. D. (2003). *Why are all the Black kids sitting together in the cafeteria? and other conversations about race.* New York: Basic Books.

Taylor, F. W. (1911). *The principles of scientific management.* New York: HarperCollins.

Terc. (2006). *Investigations in number, data, and space.* Upper Saddle River, NJ: Pearson Scott Foresman.

Tomlinson, C. (2004). *The differentiated classroom: Responding to the needs of all learners.* New York: Prentice Hall.

Troutman, D. (1999). Breaking mythical bonds: African American women's language. In R. S. Wheeler (Ed.), *The workings of language: From prescription to perspectives* (pp. 217–232). Westport, CT: Praeger.

Tyack, D. (1974). *The one best system: A history of American urban education.* Cambridge, MA: Harvard University Press.

Viadero, D. (2007). Social-skills programs found to yield gains in academic subjects. *Education Week, 27*(16), 1,15.

Vygotsky, L. S. (1978). *Mind in society.* Cambridge, MA: Harvard University Press.

Weber, L. (1991). *Inquiry, noticing, joining with, and following after.* New York: The City College Workshop Center.

Wheeler, R. S., & Swords, R. (2006). *Code-switching: Teaching standard English in urban classrooms.* Urbana, IL.: National Council of Teachers of English.

Whitehead, A. N. (1929). *The aims of education and other essays.* New York: The Free Press.

Wiggins, G. (1989). Teaching to the authentic test. *Educational Leadership, 46*(7), 41–47.

Willis, J. (2007, Summer). The neuroscience of joyful education. *Educational Leadership, 64.* Retrieved February 14, 2008, from http://www.ascd.org

Wiske, M. S. (1997). *Teaching for understanding: Linking research with practice.* San Francisco: Jossey-Bass.

Yolen, J., & Cooney, B. (1995). *Letting swift river go.* New York: Little, Brown for Young Readers.

Zaccaria, M. A. (1978). The development of historical thinking: Implications for the teaching of history. *The History Teacher, 11,* 323–340.

Zernike, K. (2000, October 23). No time for napping in today's kindergarten. *New York Times,* p. A1.

Zigler, E., Gilliam, W. S., & Jones, S. M. (2006*). A vision for universal preschool education.* New York: Cambridge University Press.

Index

About the Author

Beverly Falk is Professor and Head of the Graduate Programs in Early Childhood Education at the School of Education, The City College of the City University of New York. She has been a classroom teacher, school director, district administrator, researcher, and consultant—at the school, district, state, and national level—as well as a Fellow of the Carnegie Foundation for the Advancement of Teaching. In addition to being the editor of *The New Educator*, a quarterly journal about educator preparation published by The City College of New York's School of Education, she is the author or coauthor of numerous publications and books. These include *The Power of Questions: A Guide to Teacher and Student Research*, with Megan Blumenreich; *The Heart of the Matter: Using Standards and Assessments to Learn*; *A Teacher's Guide to Standardized Testing: Knowledge Is Power*, with Lucy Calkins and colleagues; and *Authentic Assessment in Action* (Teachers College Press, 1995), with Linda Darling-Hammond and Jacqueline Ancess.